INTEGRATING

Naturally

INTEGRATING
Naturally

Units of work for Environmental Education

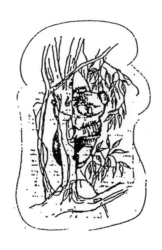

KATH MURDOCH

d

Dellasta Pty Ltd

© Kath Murdoch

First published 1992

National Library of Australia
Cataloguing-in-Publication data:

Murdoch, Kath.
    Integrating naturally: units of work for environmental
    education.

    ISBN 1 875627 21 9.

    1. Environmental education — Activity programs.
    2. conservation of natural resources — Study and teaching
    (Primary). 3. Human ecology — Study and teaching (Primary).
    I. Title.

372.357044

Illustrations by Teresa Culkin-Lawrence
Designed and typeset by Abb-typesetting Pty Ltd
126 Oxford Street, Collingwood, Victoria 3066
Printed by Brown Prior Anderson, 5 Evans Street, Burwood, Victoria 3125
Published by Dellasta Pty Ltd, 3/6 Hamilton Place,
Mount Waverley, Victoria 3149

Contents

Acknowledgements

This book would not have been possible without the assistance of many people.

I gratefully acknowledge my teachers and colleagues, Keith Pigdon and Marilyn Woolley for all they have taught me about inquiry and integrated curriculum and for their continued support, guidance and feedback. Their work has inspired many of the activities and approaches used within these units.

My special thanks to the following teachers and their students for trialling the units and providing valuable feedback:

Barbara McCoy	Northcote Primary School (Grade 3–6)
Bridget Mclaughlin	Ardeer Primary School (Grade 6)
Marg Smith	Greenbrook Primary School (Grade 3/4)
Garry Chapman	Ivanhoe Grammar School (Grade 5)
Donna Nicol	Ivanhoe Grammar School (Grade 5)
Elizabeth Barczynski	Braybrook Primary School (Grade 3)
Ruth Moodie	Braybrook Primary School (Grade 3)
Kerrie Duan	Iramoo Primary School (Grade 4)
Celia Meehan	Deer Park Primary School (Grade 3)

I also thank Jo Anne Parry and Janet Gill for their feedback and suggestions during the writing of the book; and Stephen Ray for all he has taught me about the environment and for his unfailing support and encouragement.

Finally, I wish to thank all the students who have trialled these units. It is their enthusiasm for the Earth, their desire to learn more about the environment and their willingness to make change that gives this book a purpose.

*For Sam, Adrian,
and all the other Earth
experts*

About this book

In my work as a classroom teacher and my recent experience in teacher education, I have maintained an active interest in the areas of environmental education and integrated curriculum. This book is a result of both these interests. It aims to provide teachers with a practical guide to planning integrated units of work that assist students in developing their understandings about the environment. It also offers a 'blueprint' for unit development that can be applied to other content areas, including social and science education and personal development.

The book contains five complete, integrated units of work developed around environmental topics. They are ready for use by the classroom teacher.

The units are based on the following underlying beliefs:
- that an integrated, inquiry-based curriculum can be a powerful medium through which students develop skills, values, concepts and understandings;
- that, as teachers, we have a responsibility to extend, challenge and enrich students' understanding of their world through programs that are meaningful and worthwhile;
- that in order for students to be informed decision makers who act positively *for* the environment, we should encourage a strong knowledge base *about* the environment and provide them with direct experiences *in* their environment; and
- that our teaching should empower students with knowledge about their world and about learning itself. Students should be learning how to learn and should take an active, not passive, role in the classroom.

In the past, environmental education has often been included in the curriculum in a rather 'ad hoc' manner, if at all. These units give teachers a structured, sequential approach through which to work. The integration of various curriculum areas occurs for genuine rather than artificial purposes. In this way, they offer more than a 'thematic' approach to the five topics.

This book does not offer a complete environmental education program.

The units within it, however, will make a significant contribution to a school and class program. Importantly, it will assist teachers in developing their own integrated units around topics, issues or concepts of their choice.

I hope that teachers who use these units of work in their classroom will gain as much satisfaction out of teaching them as I have had from writing and trialling them.

Kath Murdoch

The topics

Sharing the Planet ... Natural Resources

A World of their Own ... Rainforests

Around the Block ... Urban environments

An Oasis of Life ... Wetlands

On Behalf of the Other Animals ... Threatened Animals

The five unit topics have been selected for a range of reasons:

- *Students' interests*
  Each of these topics has been *successfully trialled* with students or has emerged through continued evidence of students' interest in these areas.
- *Resources*
  The five topics are *well-resourced* in terms of literature, current data, audio visual material, possible excursions etc. Resources are listed for each unit.
- *Current issues*
  Each one of these topics is of *national and international significance* and directly relevant to current social and economic contexts.
- *Variety*
  It is hoped that the selection of topics provides teachers and students with a variety of *experiences,* understandings, skills and concepts through related activities. Students have the opportunity to be engaged in inquiry and action from local through to global levels.
- *A springboard for wider learning*
  Each of the five units develop students' understandings about a particular aspect of the environment. Together, the units build broader conceptual understandings about the way the Earth works and the way humans interact with it. Connections can be made both within and between units. Themes and concepts are revisited through various units.

The 'Big Ideas' ...

Each of these units can be taught in isolation. There is no particular order in which they should be taught — you may choose to teach one or more. They are, however, linked together in that they are all related in some way to the environment and to the development of some key concepts about the relationships humans have with the environment.

The following broad understandings underpin all five units.

- Life on Earth is interconnected — living things depend on each other.
- We depend on the natural environment for our survival.
- People interact with and value the environment in different ways and for different reasons.
- The lifestyles of humans have put many pressures on the natural environment.
- There are ways we can all modify our lifestyle in order to better ensure the health of the planet.
- Environmental issues are often characterised by a conflict of interest.
- The natural environment is a source of learning and of fun, creativity, relaxation and adventure.

Why environmental topics?

From my teaching and the trialling of these units, it is clear that teachers and students alike find much fascination, interest and enjoyment in environmental inquiry. This reaction is an excellent basis on which to develop many important learning skills.

Environmental education is rapidly becoming a significant part of the school curriculum. As the world experiences increasing effects of poor environmental management, we are learning that environmental ignorance can have far-reaching ramifications for the Earth and all its inhabitants.

People need to be environmentally literate and environmental education is one way we can help ensure that future generations will be well-informed and have a clearer understanding of the way their Earth works. As a result of environmental education, we hope that people will actively pursue a lifestyle that protects rather than damages the environment.

Not just about the environment

These five units are not only designed to develop students' knowledge and understanding of the environment. The teaching strategies suggested throughout also develop skills such as those for co-operative learning, decision making, researching, solving problems and creative thinking.

An integrated curriculum perspective

A systematically planned, integrated curriculum can do much for the development of students' understandings about and feelings for the environment. However, the curriculum must be *genuinely* rather than artificially integrated. These units utilise a range of curriculum areas but do so in meaningful and purposeful ways. Not all curriculum areas are used in each one — only those that seem appropriate.

Thinking about the 'whats' before the 'hows'

It is important that we have clear in our minds *what* it is that we hope students will learn through a unit of work on any topic. Good unit planning evolves from a consideration of the content with which students will be engaged — it is this content that should drive our subsequent planning. This consideration takes time. It is more than an enthusiastic scramble to find songs and poems about trees. It is through talking with others, reading relevant literature, seeking out resources and exploring existing activity ideas that teachers can decide on a set of understandings that will guide their planning.

Once we are clear about what it is that we are hoping students will come to understand, we can then select experiences and processes that will assist them in sorting out and coming to conclusions about the topic. It is this real knowledge and understanding that helps empower students to act for the environment. Their actions are born of reflection on knowledge gained.

In designing integrated units about the environment, we should be planning activities that encourage students to explore, gather, process, refine and present information about the environment.

In the following units, most of the planning has already been done for you. You need simply to make decisions about the activities that are most appropriate for the needs and interests of your students.

Approaches to Teaching and Learning

The units have been developed using an *inquiry* approach to teaching and learning and, where appropriate, they *integrate* a variety of curriculum areas.

The teaching strategies suggested within each unit are designed to provide students with a definite structure within which to investigate. This structure allows students to make some decisions about the things they will focus on and about the ways they may go about finding out or presenting information. At the same time, your role is clear. You are more than a 'guide' — you play an active role in setting directions, designing a range of activities, organising groupings and implementing a *sequence* of learning experience appropriate for your students.

The units: how to use them most effectively

Each of the five units of work follows a similar sequence. The sequence is an inquiry-based one that encourages students to gather and process information and to reflect and act upon what they have learned. The stages below are provided for each unit.

- *Rationale*
  This section provides some background information for you about the topic and the relevance of it to the students and to the environment.

- *Contents*
  At the beginning of each unit an outline is provided to give you an overview of the sequence of all activities and experiences within the unit.

- *About this unit*
  This section gives you a general idea of the purposes and characteristics of the particular unit.

- *Understandings*
  These statements are designed to clarify the direction the unit will take. The understandings are a list of what it is that the students and you will be working towards, i.e what could be considered as important to know about the topic. They are also a useful evaluation device.

- *Key concepts*
  These are the broad ideas that students will be developing and clarifying. Again, they assist you in selecting activities and evaluating students' progress. The concepts in each unit are important concepts for environmental education in general.

- *Skills*
  A list is provided in each unit of the skills that will be learnt or practised through the various unit activities.

- *Sample unit planner*
  This planner offers one way of organising and sequencing the unit. It includes a selection of activities from each stage and shows how they might be organised over six weeks.

The activities

Stage 1 — Tuning in

Activities are suggested here simply to get students engaged in thinking about the topic. They are designed to **sensitise and motivate** students ... to get the ball rolling.

Stage 2 — Preparing to find out

These activities are designed with three main aims:
1. To give you some insight into **what the students already know** about the topic and where their initial interests lie.
2. To help students focus clearly on what they already know and **what they will try to find out**. Some activities require the students to make decisions about the ways they will go about gathering information.
3. To **prepare the students for the experience to follow** (e.g. an excursion) and to focus their investigations.

Stage 3 — Finding out

For each unit, a selection of shared experiences is suggested from which you may choose one or two. These experiences are usually direct — outdoor excursions are emphasised. The experiences are designed to give students the opportunity to gather new information about a topic.

Stage 4 — Sorting out

In this stage a variety of activities is suggested across **a wide range of curriculum areas** such as art, language, maths, drama, music and movement. Here, students will process information they have gathered and present it in a number of different ways. They may also begin to draw some conclusions about what it is they have learnt. They usually begin with more concrete curriculum areas (such as art) and move to the more abstract (such as written language).

Stage 5 — Going further

This selection of activities is designed to **challenge and extend** students' understanding about the topic. They will often bring new information to the unit or suggest related activities that could extend from the major sequence.

Stage 6 — Making connections

At this stage, students will be drawing **conclusions about what they have learnt.** This is an important time for you to evaluate the success of the unit and the needs and achievements of individuals. This is where students put it all together.

Stage 7 — Taking action

This is a very important element of both the inquiry process and of environmental education. It is important that students be given opportunities to **act upon what they have learnt.** A variety of actions is suggested, most of which centre around the student's life and home. They are things that students can do themselves and from which they can see results.

Black Line Masters

These are provided at the end of each unit. They are designed to be used **in conjunction with the unit** rather than as separate, one-off activity sheets; however, many could be used in that way. The unit sequence indicates the most appropriate times to use the BLMs.

You may well ask . . .

For whom are the units intended?

These units have been written for use in the middle to upper primary school. They have been trialled with students in grades 3 to 6 in both single and multi-age classrooms in a variety of physical and social settings. Many activities are also suitable for lower, post-primary students.

Should I do all the activities?

At each stage of the unit, a number of activities are listed. You would not be expected to do them all. Instead, the units are designed so that a selection of activities can be made at each stage. You should select the activities according to the needs and interests of your students and the time and resources available to you.

While you are encouraged to follow the suggested inquiry sequence for each topic, it is quite possible to pick and choose from the range of activity ideas throughout the book. These may be used in conjunction with other programs.

How do these units fit into my weekly program?

Although these units integrate a range of curriculum areas, they are not designed to be a total program. It is assumed that the regular routines that operate in your classroom will continue to run alongside your unit work.

For example, you may have regular times for process writing, project maths, a literature program etc. These things don't change — although at times students' writing topics or choice of books may be influenced or directed by the current unit.

How long should each unit run?

This will of course depend very much on your particular school, classroom and students. Generally though, the units seem to run for about six weeks.

I don't know much about these topics myself — will I be able to teach them effectively?

Yes! The units are designed in such a way that you, as the teacher, are given most of the information that you need to carry out the activities. You

SAMPLE TIMETABLE FOR ONE WEEK OF "WETLANDS UNIT"

	9:00	9:45 — Language	11:00 — Maths	1:30 — Current Unit Focus: ENVIRONMENTAL EDUCATION TOPIC: Wetlands	2:30 — ENVIRONMENTAL EDUCATION
MONDAY	Whole grade meeting time: community activities (aerobics, singing, stories etc.)	Language Workshop • Conferences • Clinics	Maths Workshop (Focus: measuring temperatures) • project maths groups	Unit Work — Meet in small groups to share data gathered from excursion	ART — Unit work. Initial response to excursion using wet paper & chalk.
TUESDAY		Language Workshop • Conferences • Clinics	Maths Workshop • Project Maths groups	Unit Work (Drama) Values Clarification "In another pair of Shoes" Interviews in role. / {Music}	Unit Work (Language) Conflict Matrix "Living with Wetlands" List key words & add to word banks.
WEDNESDAY		{Library} Using factual materials to research wetland animals	Activity Maths (In maths task centre) Parents and Community helpers	{Italian}	Unit work Planning our Wetlands. "What do we need?" Listing & drawing
THURSDAY		Literature program. Group 1 Flat Stanley; Group 2 Gilly Hopkins; Group 3 Bernice Knows Best; Group 4 Down Round-a-bott and Up Again	Whole grade maths focus & Automatic response / {Italian}	Unit Work. Work in small groups. • Rotate through. Setting up various components. Jointly constructed procedural text "How to build a wetland"	groups. wetland area
FRIDAY		Handwriting / writing. Re-work procedural texts in small groups — write up "rules for wetlands" for display	Maths & Unit Work. Denise observation tasks for wetlands. What will we monitor? How will we record changes?	Reflective journal writing on unit activities. Individual Catch-up work.	{Sport} / {Phys. Ed.}

LANGUAGE FOCUS: MODELLING REPORT WRITING / SPELLING PARTNERS

SHARE TIME: PRESENTING WORK IN PROGRESS, SINGING: POEMS: CHANTS — RECESS

SHARE TIME: PRESENTING WORK IN PROGRESS MATHS GAMES & PROBLEMS / SERIAL: THE MAGIC FINGER, by ROALD DAHL / CLASS

are provided with background notes when necessary and the resources listed are readily available. Extra reading and discussion with other staff about the topic will enhance your teaching. Most importantly, though, you will find that you learn with the students and make discoveries with them. When you are unsure about something . . . use it as an opportunity to demonstrate ways of finding out.

For assistance in planning your own units, see pp 183.

How will I find the time to fit it all in?

The units will offer opportunities to integrate your weekly program perhaps more closely than at present. For example, students may construct graphs after a visit to a wetland — this could be legitimately done as part of your maths program. They may be writing letters to find out information about rainforests — why not make this a handwriting session as well? You will give students a much greater purpose for improving the quality of their handwriting and will be pursuing a meaningful activity at the same time. All this leads to a more economical use of time and a holistic program that makes better sense to you and your students.

The sample weekly timetable on page 10 may give you some ideas about incorporating these integrated units into your weekly program.

Routines such as language and maths workshops and literature programs remain 'fixed' in the weekly timetable. However, where appropriate, the unit content may be utilised in these sessions. In this sample week, report writing is the language focus because it will assist children with their own wetland reports later in the unit.

Similarly, 'unit' activities will help children develop skills in a range of curriculum areas, such as graphing and measuring water levels in the wetland, which should be regarded as much as an exercise in maths as it is a unit activity. (These links will not always occur.)

The unit should not be your whole program. Specialists may take up the unit. In this case, art and library play an important role in the 'sorting out' phase of the activity sequence.

The afternoon content in this timetable depends very much on the unit itself. Curriculum areas focused on could be checked off on a record sheet to ensure a balance across the term and year.

An integrated timetable does not mean that we lose structure in our programs. It does, however, recognise that children should be using a range of processes at various times in a week, to sort out information and present their understandings. The *content* will determine some of your week's timetable; ongoing routines will determine the rest.

Try sharing the timetable for each week with your students — get them to plan *with* you — this is another way we can help children feel more engaged in, and responsible for, their learning.

Record-keeping and evaluation

Evaluation should be seen as an ongoing process and should blend in rather than be 'tacked on' to your units.

These integrated units have been designed to include evaluation strategies throughout the teaching sequence. There are activities within each stage that are useful for assessing the growth in understandings or skills that students are achieving through the unit.

It is particularly important to observe students working at the **'Making Connections'** stage. Activities such as concept mapping, futures wheels, statement writing etc. are all ways that students are asked to demonstrate specifically what they have learnt.

Skills

A checklist comprising many of the skills referred to in the units is included for your convenience. This could be used when planning your own units of work or as a record-keeping / observation sheet to document students' development.

Understandings

The understandings at the beginning of each unit provide you with a useful reference point for observation. As students demonstrate those understandings to you in some way, anecdotal or formal notes can be made.

It is not expected that all students will reach all understandings in any unit. They will come to them at their own pace and in different ways.

Skills checklist

Below is a list of some of the skills that are practised across the five units.
You may find this a useful guide when **selecting activities for your own units** or as a **checklist for observing students.**

Skills

- **Gathering information**
- **Representing data**
- **Using factual texts as references**
- **Co-operating**
- **Clarifying values**
- **Empathising**
- **Presenting a point of view**
- **Actively listening**
- **Making decisions**
- **Solving problems**
- **Predicting**
- **Imagining**
- **Taking action**
- **Classifying**
- **Reporting (oral and written)**
- **Logical thinking**
- **Gathering data**
- **Interpreting data**
- **Observing**
- **Creating**
- **Comparing**
- **Questioning**
- **Recording**

Self-evaluation

It is important to involve students in this evaluation by encouraging them to reflect on their own learning during the unit. Re-visiting the ideas that they had at the beginning of the unit and comparing them with later understandings is one way we can help students reflect on and celebrate their learning.

Students can provide us with useful feedback about their own development and about the success or otherwise of the activities we provide.

The black line masters below are provided to assist students in self-assessment and evaluation of the units.

Unit Evaluation Sheet

Unit topic: _____

My favourite part of the unit was _____

because _____

_____

I didn't enjoy _____

because _____

Three things I have learnt are:

1. _____

_____

2. _____

_____

3. _____

_____

I would still like to know more about: _____

_____

Other comments about the unit: _____

_____

Signed _____

Date _____

Thinking about my work

Name _____

Unit _____

1. During this unit, I have worked:

Poorly_____ extremely well.
(Mark the spot on the line)

2. As a group member, I have been:

Unco-operative_____ very co-operative.
(Mark the spot on the line)

3. Looking back over my work, I am most proud of: _____

4. I have got better at:_____

_____

5. I still need to work on: _____

_____

Signed _____ Date_____

Record-keeping

Good record-keeping helps us evaluate and provides a medium through which we can share students' learning with other teachers, parents and the community. Some examples of record-keeping ideas are as follows:

Compile a class journal or scrap book for each unit to which individuals or groups may contribute. This journal may contain:

- newspaper articles with commentaries;
- reflections on observations, news items;
- ideas, poems, comments on issues arising from unit;
- copies of BLMs, wall stories, particular pieces of work;
- photos and captions.

This will provide a useful record of the unit for you, the class and the school community.

Students may have individual journals about the topic in which they can store their own work throughout the unit.

Exercise or scrapbooks can be used as 'topic books'.

For every unit that students do, they have a topic book in which they store individual work.

Ask the students to begin to observe any changes they notice in their own and their peers' environmental habits. Keep a list of these in the classroom.

Collect relevant samples of work that demonstrate the development of understandings. Store these in individual student files.

Keep all wall charts, lists etc. One way of doing this is to clip them to labelled hangers which can be suspended in the room. Another is to make large, sturdy card pockets for work from each unit.

Students should have access to these resources throughout the year.

Compile photo albums of unit activities and pieces of work with captions written by students to go home to parents.

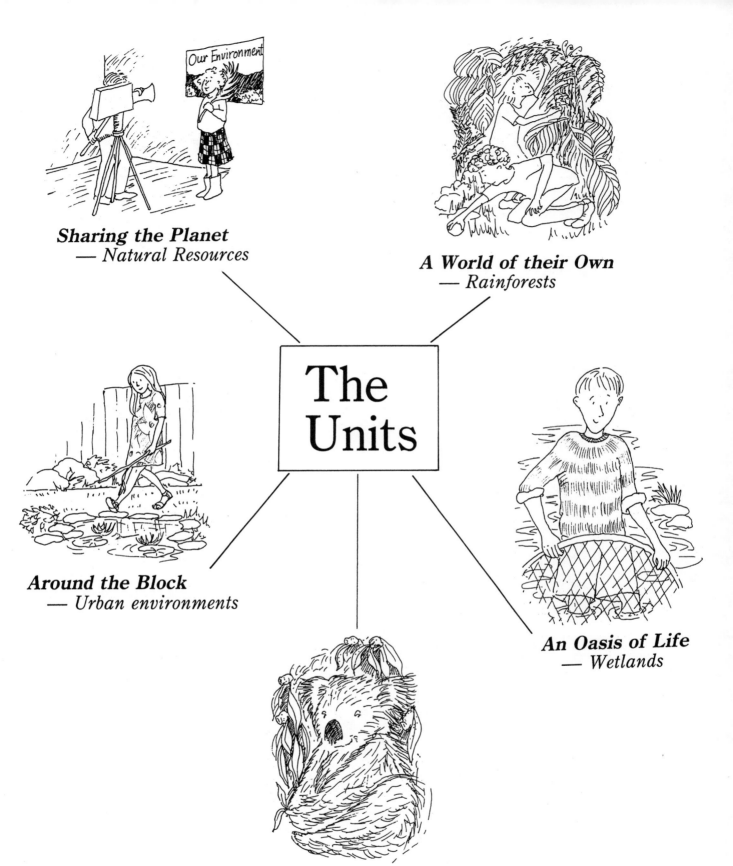

Sharing the Planet
— *Natural Resources*

A World of their Own
— *Rainforests*

Around the Block
— *Urban environments*

The Units

An Oasis of Life
— *Wetlands*

On Behalf of the Other Animals
— *Threatened Animals*

Sharing the Planet

An integrated unit of work about nature's resources

Rationale

All the amazing things that humans create exist because of the Earth's natural resources. Our clothing, shelter, food, transport etc. are all ultimately derived from the Earth — from its rocks and minerals, water, air, plants and animals.

We use nature's resources to satisfy our needs and our wants. Changes in our lifestyle and the growth of technology have increased the pressure we place on many of these natural resources — and, although they may seem bountiful, they are indeed finite. We are often unaware of our dependence on natural resources — simply because we rarely 'see' the natural origin of our many modern conveniences. The supermarket shelf provides us only with the final product and thus masks the true source of the things we consume.

There is an increasing need to develop lifestyles and habits that sustain rather than deplete the Earth's resources. We are but one life form among many millions of others with whom we share the planet. Our survival is linked to their survival and the maintenance of the Earth's atmosphere, waters and soils. Our use of nature's resources is often unnecessarily wasteful or damaging. There are many simple things that students and adults alike can do to reduce their impact on the planet. Reducing consumption, re-using and recycling materials are just some ways in which we can develop more 'Earth-friendly' habits and help sustain resources for all life.

Contents

The list below is a summary of the activities that you will find in this unit.
It is not suggested that you do them all but that you select some activities
from under each major heading to suit your purposes.

Then you know
that although it is only a little planet
it is hugely beautiful
and surely the finest place in the world
to be.

So watch it, look at it
see what it's like
to walk around on it.

It's small but it's beautiful
it's small but it's fine
like a rainbow,

like a bubble.

— Lawrence Collins;

About this unit

This unit of work is designed to develop broad understandings about the Earth's natural resources, their finite nature and the impact that humans have on them. The unit revolves around the book *The Lorax* by Dr Seuss (although any general book or video that explores environmental degradation may be suitable). Beginning with activities that encourage students to explore their perception of the Earth and the things that make it up, the sequence moves towards the consideration of change in our personal lifestyles.

Understandings:

- The Earth's natural resources are finite.
- Natural resources are both living and non-living.
- All living things depend on these resources for their survival.
- Impact on a resource can lead to impact on many living things that depend on that resource.
- People use natural resources in a variety of ways for a variety of purposes.
- People everywhere have a similar range of needs for their survival. We also have a range of material wants that are not essential for survival.
- The imbalance between human needs and wants can explain much of the Earth's environmental degradation.
- There are many things that we can do as individuals that will help reduce the stresses on the Earth.

Key concepts

Natural/human-made   Change
Inter-relationships   Needs and wants
Cause and effect   Finite/infinite

Skills

Observing
Clarifying values   Presenting a point of view
Gathering information   Listening
Representing data   Decision making
Researching using factual materials   Problem solving
Co-operating   Questioning

Comments:

SHARING THE PLANET – SAMPLE UNIT PLANNER

	Session 1	Session 2	Session 3	Session 4	Session 5	Ongoing Activities
Week 1	TUNING IN • Let's go shopping • Time Capsules	• Outdoor listening and looking • Classification activity BLMs 1&2	• Picture book "Giant" • The Earth making statements	PREPARING TO FIND OUT • What are natural resources	• Earth wheels BLM 3	• Children reflect on activities & learning in personal journals
Week 2	• Webbing game • Making an earth model	• Concept mapping BLM 4	• Revisit work so far • What do we know?	• Video • The Lorax • Small groups focus on one aspect.	• Initial response to video • Cross group sharing	• Collect relevant articles & pictures from newspaper. Class journal
Week 3	SORTING OUT Art • Before and after murals	DRAMA • Role-play BLMs 5&6	• Role play continued • Debriefing	Language • Letters • Flip Book	GOING FURTHER • Needs & wants activity Part A	• Individual research into one resource. Use of library
Week 4	Needs & wants activity	MAKING CONNECTIONS • Revisit Earth wheel • Writing statements	• Resequencing statements • Begin class Big Book	• Continue Big Book	Re-do concept map for evaluation	• Word list to develop from activities. Use words in spelling program.
Week 5	• Presentations of individual projects on a specific resource	• Presentations continued	• Model a futures wheel – whole class	• Individual futures wheels for evaluation	TAKING ACTION • Brainstorm personal action to reduce impact on resources BLM 7	• Read general picture story books on the environment
Week 6	Actions for specific resources	• Completed individual pledges BLM 8	• Whole class action – decide as a group BLM 9	• Carrying out action (this will depend on children's choice)	• Unit evaluation and reflection	• Collect relevant samples for files.

Tuning In →
Preparing to find out →
Finding out →
Sorting Out →
Going Further →
Making Connections →
Taking Action →

Tuning in

The activities suggested here are designed simply to get students engaged in thinking about the topic. They are designed to sensitise and motivate students . . . to 'get the ball rolling.'

Let's go shopping!

Bring in a string shopping bag with a range of food and household items, e.g.

- a tin of fruit;
- a box of soap;
- a packet of ham;
- a bottle of tomato sauce;
- a plastic container;
- a cotton T-shirt;
- a can of mineral water;
- a ball of wool;
- a shampoo;
- a block of chocolate etc.

Tell the students that you have just been shopping. Ask them where they think everything came from. The shop? . . . Yes . . . but what about before that?

Give items to pairs or small groups. They must discuss, together, how they think that item, packaging included, was made and where it came from. List ideas.

Note that the range of origins is much more limited than the range of product types (e.g. many of these things came from animals, plants or minerals). You will come back to this concept later — but you should have the students pretty interested now!

An Earth time capsule

Ask the students to imagine what they might put in a time capsule for the Earth if they knew it was about to be destroyed.

'What could we put in the capsule that would show what the earth is like to someone who might discover our capsule millions of years from now?' (You might limit the number of items to say, five.)

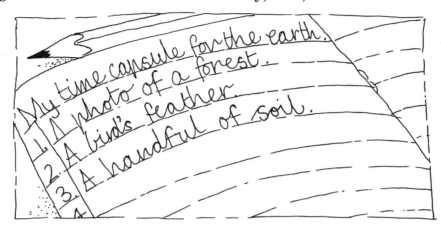

Getting out there

Go outside into the school yard. Using BLM 1 (p. 43) students list the things that they hear and see. They then try to organise these things in lists under the headings 'natural' and 'human-made' using the BLM 2 (p. 44).

Ask students to share their ideas in small groups.

Talking it over

Follow the previous activity with a discussion of the terms 'natural' and 'human-made'.

'What are some of the natural things that we saw? Are there any natural things in this classroom?

What does human-made mean? Is a wooden bench natural or human-made?

Picture story books

Read books with a general environmental focus such as *'Giant'* by Juliet and Charles Snape (Julia Macrae, 1989). (See resource list on page 42)

Preparing to find out

These activities are designed with three main aims:

1. To give you some insight into what the students already know about the topic and where their initial interests lie.
2. To help students focus clearly on what they already know and what they will try to find out. Some activities require the students to make decisions about the ways they will go about gathering information.
3. To prepare the students for the experience to follow (e.g. an excursion) and to focus their investigations.

What do you know . . . ?

Provide students with a broad focus question, e.g. 'What do you know about the Earth?' This can be done by standing the students in a big circle. They throw a ball representing the Earth to each other. When they catch the ball, they complete the sentence, 'The Earth . . . '

After some discussion, students may write their ideas individually, in small groups or as a class. Students who are unable to write theirs down may be able to get another student or a teacher to do it for them. These statements can then be classified into groups according to the topic that they deal with. Highlight important words within the sentence to begin developing a 'bank' of words related to the environment in general.

The Earth is a planet.
The Earth has living things on it.

What are natural resources?

In pairs, write down what you think natural resources are. Have a class discussion and try to come up with a class definition of natural resources.

Divide class up into five groups. Each group brainstorms their ideas about how we use one of the following resources: rocks and minerals; water; animals; plants; air.

They then represent their ideas visually.

Discuss the question, 'Are humans natural resources?'

Earthwheels

Introduce the BLM 3 (p. 45). In each segment, students draw or write responses to the following:

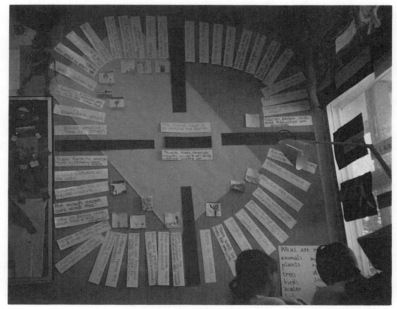

- Things on the Earth that are abundant.

- Things on the Earth that are scarce.

- Ways we harm the environment.

- Ways we help the environment.

Students share their Earth wheels. Information is discussed, challenged and refined.

Class constructs a giant Earth wheel.

The webbing game

This game explores a basic concept about the environment and can help students express their initial understandings. Students take on the role of different plants, animals and other natural resources and show the way these things are interrelated by connecting with each other using a ball of string.

Below are some words that you might use for the webbing game. Write them on cards and fix to students' clothing using pins or sticky labels.

sun	soil	human	eagle	lizard
tree	water	dingo	worm	sand
caterpillar	fish	possum	ant	goanna
magpie	air	grass	rocks	

An Earth model

This activity and the following ones are designed to have students think about three key concepts: the finite nature of natural resources; the 'interconnectedness' of these things; and human impact on resources.

A useful activity to get students thinking about Earth is to attempt to make a model of it. Examine pictures of the Earth, world maps and look at a globe of the Earth.

Discuss: Where is the Earth in space? What is it *made* of? What *shape* is it? If the Earth is made of land and water, what is the proportion of each?

Problem solving activity: try and work out the ratio of water to land. What other natural things would we need to show? (land, air, water, animals and plants.) How could we show these in a model? What do we need?

If we had to make a model of the Earth to explain what it is like to a creature from another planet, what would be important to show?

In small groups, design an Earth model. Write an explanatory caption for your model. Share and discuss the various models that the students have made.

Below is one example of an Earth model. To make it, use soil and water in a sand tray. Cover with wire and then plastic wrap to simulate the atmosphere. Condensation will occur showing the way the water cycle works. Seeds planted in the soil model the growth of plants. Keep a daily observation diary for observations of the Earth model.

(Source: Stapp, W. and Cox, D. *Environmental Education Activities Manual* Stapp and Cox, 1974.)

A concept map

This activity can be done in a variety of ways. Two ways are suggested below.

1. Students are given the sheet of word cards on BLM 4 (p. 46) and asked to arrange these in a way that makes sense to them and shows how they are connected.

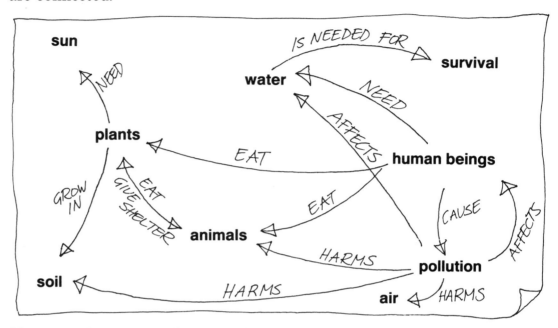

2. Alternatively, you could ask students to write down ten words that they think of when they think about the Earth. They then use their words to construct a concept map in the same way as shown above.

Students share their concept map with the class or with a small group then store it for future reference and revision.

Finding out

These experiences are designed to give students the opportunity to gather new information about the topic.

Revising

Bring students together to revise what you've done so far. Refer to charts, concept maps, Earth wheels and models. Refer to original statements about the Earth. Are there statements that we wish to change? What do we need to find out more about?

Independent research

During library time or for homework throughout the unit, students could investigate one particular resource and present information to the group throughout the unit. Some examples are trees, a mineral such as iron, sand, water etc.

Encourage students to list some focus questions to guide their project. Below are some examples:

- What type of resource is it?
- Where it is found?
- What it is used for?
- How it is manufactured?
- What are the environmental effects of using it?

Encourage students to use resource material such as the non-fiction texts listed at the end of this unit. After students have gathered information, they could present it in any way they wish, such as in an oral, visual or written format.

The Lorax *by Dr. Seuss — a shared experience*

This video of the popular Dr Seuss book, *The Lorax* provides an excellent overview of environmental destruction in relation to the wants of human beings. Human impact on plants, animals, air, water and soil is explored through the lively tale of the greedy Mr Once-ler. The message of hope at the end of the story is an excellent springboard to action at the conclusion of the unit.

Other suitable shared experiences would be any general videos that deal with environmental degradation, or a visit from a guest speaker from groups in the resource list such as the Environment Protection Authority or the Australian Conservation Foundation.

One way to help the students focus on the information in the video is to divide the grade up and ask groups to focus on one particular resource (air, water, land, plants, animals). During the video, students note all the ways in which it is damaged.

Another way is to give the grade some general focus question to have in mind when they watch the video, e.g. 'As you watch the video, list all the ways that you see the natural environment being affected.'

Sorting out

A variety of activities is suggested across a range of curriculum areas. Students will process information they have gathered and present it in a number of different ways. They may also begin to draw some conclusions about what it is they have learnt.

Sharing notes

Students meet in small groups after watching the video in the activity above. Each group should consist of individuals who took notes about different resources. Discuss the things that were written down.

Art

After watching or listening to *The Lorax*, the students can express their responses and understandings through art. Some suggested approaches can be found below.

Painting

Paint something that shows ways that the Once-ler had an impact on the environment.

Models — before and after

Build a model that shows the way the land looked before the Once-ler came to town and then another model to show how it looked afterwards.

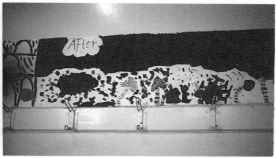

Comic strips

Students re-tell the story by making comic strip–type representations of the sequence of events. This may be done with or without speech balloons and captions.

Group work

Students may get into the groups according to the resource on which they were focussing and present the impact on that resource through art.

The activity may be less structured. Say something like, 'I would like you to decide as a group about one thing that you think was important from the video. Tell the rest of us about it using any of the materials that I have put out.'

Drama

The drama activities below could be used to process further the information gained through the shared experience.

Role play

BLMs 5 and 6 (pp. 47 & 48) are based on the story of *The Lorax* and can be used for a role play activity.

1. Read the newspaper article with students and discuss.
2. Allocate roles to individuals in the class by numbering them off from one to five.

1. Mr Once-ler

2. Mr Lorax

3. Ms Barbaloot

4. Ms O Funs-ler

5. Councillor

Groups made up of students with the same numbers and therefore the same roles meet to discuss and prepare their response to the problem.

Students prepare to take on their particular role by discussing how they think their character would feel and the arguments they will present to the public meeting.

New groups of five, with a representative of the numbers 1–5, then meet to discuss the problem (the public meeting) and try to come to some agreements. Each group elects a chairperson to conduct the meeting.

If the members of the class cannot be divided equally into fives, there will obviously be two of some characters in some groups.

Share the outcomes of the meetings and the feelings of individuals in role.

Documentaries

Students work in groups to devise short, documentary-style presentations that explain an aspect of the story, e.g. the loss of habitat for the Barbaloot bears. These could be combined with some art and music and video-taped.

Formal debate

This is similar to the role play although here students present their arguments in a formal debate setting. Groups can be those 'for', those 'against', an arbitration group to monitor proceedings and research groups to assist each side with the development of their argument.

Mime

This can be a powerful way to express experience. Students could develop short, silent scenarios in relation to *The Lorax*. They may take on different roles (an animal, ranger, visitor, student) and mime the same scene from various characters' perspectives.

Debriefing

Drama is an excellent way for students to explore issues about the environment. It gives them a chance to find out about the feelings and values that other people have and, in doing so, to further clarify their own feelings and values.

Given that the activities often bring about necessary conflict, it is important that students have the opportunity to talk about how they felt during the activity and what they learnt about the characters and the issues. Questions that you might ask during the debriefing are:

- How did you feel about having to be someone else?
- Did you agree with your character?
- What did your character feel? Why?
- Who felt uncomfortable during the role play? Why?
- Who felt good? Why?
- Whose arguments were convincing? Why?

Language

Initial responses to **The Lorax**

Encourage students to write about *The Lorax* in the following ways:

- Write the story in a range of styles or for a range of audiences
- A mock diary of one of the characters in the book/video.

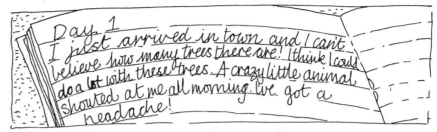

- A newspaper article — similar to the example in BLM 5.
- An advertisement for the now vacant factory equipment.

- A summary of the main events for a historical text book.
- An alternative ending for the story.
- A story map that shows the sequence of events.
- A letter to Mr Once-ler.

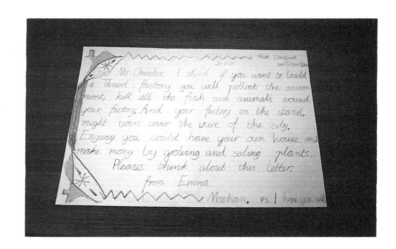

Listing

A variety of lists can be made following the shared experience.

These lists can be made by individuals, pairs or small groups and are a way of sorting out the information gained through the shared experience as well as further adding to the 'bank' of topic words around the room.

'List all of the actions that humans did that damaged the environment.

Now group all the things that belong together. Can we add to these lists by looking around our school or wider community?'

Flip book

Students construct sentences with the structure: Preposition Adjective Subject Verb Adverb Setting (prepositional phrase), such as: 'The angry Lorax yelled loudly in the Once-ler's office' and 'Some sick swans flew silently into the smog.'

Using the same structure, write sentences on cards that can be mixed up to create crazy sentences.

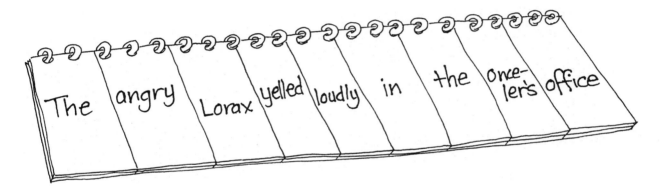

Going further

These activities are designed to challenge and extend students' understandings about the topic.

Needs and wants

At this stage in the unit, it is suggested that you take some time to explore the concept of needs and wants with the students. The activity below takes a light-hearted look at needs and wants but successfully engages students in discussion and debate and clarification of the main ideas.

The teacher proposes the following: 'You are locked alone in a large department store that sells just about everything you could possibly imagine. You decide to take anything you want (except money) regardless of price, size etc.' Give students about five minutes to write a list, then share some of the ideas.

'OK . . . unfortunately you've been caught out. In payment for your crime, all your money and material possessions have been taken away from you. All you have are the things that you took from the store.'

'You are allowed to keep 5 of the things on your list. You will need to think about your survival. Is anything on your list going to be of use? . . . not much?'

'All right, let's change the fantasy. You've lost everything. Your home, your money, your possessions. Someone takes pity on you and you are given the chance to go back into the store and select ten things that you need. What will you choose? Is there anything that you need that this or any other shop doesn't have? Talk to the others at your tables before you decide.'

'Now, together, make a list of these "needs". What is the difference between needs and wants? There is sure to be some argument about the necessity of some items. This should illustrate the notion that needs and wants are perceived quite differently by individuals.

'What about the things that you couldn't buy?'

Application

To reinforce the students' understandings, use magazine pictures to complete the following task: Find pictures that illustrate the following-

- Things you need
- Things that you want — and couldn't really cope without (e.g. a fridge to preserve food)
- Things that you want but could comfortably survive without (e.g. a television).

Discussion: Why are our 'wants' different? What are 'reasonable' wants? Why are people's wants different? What do you consider to be reasonable wants?

Students, in pairs, select one item that they agree is a need and one item that they agree is a want. They then discuss what impact the use of each of those two things has on the environment. Give each pair the following focus questions to explore with their two items:

- What is used to make the item?
- Where does it come from?
- Does the thing affect the environment in any way when you use it?

Ask students what they have learnt about needs and wants.

Making connections

At this stage, students will be drawing conclusions about what they have learnt. This is an important time for you to evaluate the success of the unit and the needs and achievements of individuals. This is where students put it all together.

Revisiting

Provide students with a selection of focus areas. They may be the same ones you used at the beginning of the unit for the Earth wheel activity:

- Resources on the Earth that are abundant.
- Resources on the Earth that are scarce.
- Ways we harm the environment.
- Ways we help the environment.

Ask students whether they can now add to the list above.

Statements

Ask students to write some statements about natural resources. Give them these questions as prompts:

- What do you know about natural resources?
- What do you know about needs and wants?
- What do you know about natural and human-made things?
- What do you know about the Earth?

Our wants do most harm to the earth. (Kate)

Natural resources are finite (Mario)

The earth is a planet in space (Ben)

Students may draft personal statements and then make collective lists in groups. Allow time for the students to challenge and question each other's statements.

These statements can be used for a range of language activities such as:

- covering words for a whole class cloze activity;
- writing them out on cards, cutting them up, then asking each other to re-sequence them.

- use them as the basis of a big book — The Earth. The book can then be read to other grades and parents at home.

Statements should be compared to the ideas and questions that the students had at the beginning of the unit.

What have we learnt? How have our ideas changed?

Concept mapping

Conduct the concept mapping activity again without showing the originals to students. Afterwards show students the originals and ask, 'How are they different? What have we learnt?'

Futures wheels

Students create a futures wheel based on one natural resource.

Other starters could be:

- more recycling;
- less clean water;
- less air pollution.

Personal projects

Allow time for students to work on their individual or group project about a resource (see 'independent research' above). When they are ready, their ideas should be presented to the class.

Taking action

This is a very important element of both the inquiry process and of environmental education. It is essential that students be given opportunities to act upon what they have learnt.

The focus now shifts from the way humans cause environmental degradation to the way we can prevent and heal unnecessary degradation of natural resources. This is an enormous area and can be inaccessible for students. It is best to focus on what they can do.

This unit has a general focus on natural resources so one way to begin discussion on action is to get students to brainstorm things they can do to help conserve each broad resource area (water, air, soil, plants and animals) BLM 7 (p. 49) gives students a guide for their brainstorming. Students could complete this activity in pairs. There are a range of publications that outline very simple things that we can do to look after the natural environment. These texts should be made available to students during this activity. (Refer to resource list.)

Share ideas for personal action as a class. Students then select three things that they think they could do as an individual. When they have decided, they complete the 'Earth Pledge' BLM 8 (p. 50) sheet. These sheets can be coloured and displayed in the room.

BLM 9 (p. 51) can be used by the whole grade in a similar way to the above and displayed in the school.

Some ideas for simple, personal action are: walking or riding instead of driving to school; bringing lunch in a lunch box that can be re-used every day; refusing plastic bags at the supermarket — use string bags or baskets; using both sides of paper.

Examples of class action are suggested below:

- Become involved in some sort of environmental improvement in the school ground or at a local site, e.g. tree planting, weeding, setting up a compost heap.
- Establish a paper, can or bottle recycling program in the school.
- Write letters to the newspaper, to an organisation, to a local politician, to the school council.
- Publish an article in the school newsletter.
- Give talks to other grades or schools.
- Set up information displays at a local community centre (e.g. library, bank).
- Devise personal action contracts that will be carried out at home — changing habits or forming new ones.

All actions should be monitored and discussed regularly. Students should be given the opportunity to talk about how easy or difficult the actions are and perhaps to modify their pledges if necessary. Above all, the actions should be achievable and celebrated. Perhaps environmental awards could be given at school assembly times to those people whom your students deem to be worthy recipients!

Resources

Fiction

Baylor, B *Everybody needs a Rock* Alladin 1974

Foreman, M *Dinosaurs and all that Rubbish* Puffin 1972

Ingpen, R and Dunkle, M *Conservation: A Thoughtful Way of Explaining Conservation to Children* Hill of Content 1987

Oodgeroo, N and Noonucul, K *The Rainbow Serpent* AGPS 1988

Peet, B *The Wump World* Houghton Mifflin 1970

Dr Seuss *The Lorax* Collins 1971

Snape, J and C *Giant* Julie Macrae 1989

Martinez C (ed.) *Once upon a Planet: An Anthology of Stories and Extracts* Puffin 1988

Van Essen, S A *Wilderness Story* Zoe Community School Tasmania 1984

Walker K *Father Sky and Mother Earth* Jacaranda 1981

Non-Fiction

Breidahl, H *Ecology: The Story of Life, the Earth and Everything* Macmillan 1987

Drew, David *Millions of Years Ago* Nelson (Informazing) 1988

Gamlin, L *Life on Earth* (Today's World Series) Alladin 1988

Houghton, G and Wakefield, J *The Natural Environment* (Australian Picture Library) Macmillan 1985

Jennings, T *The Earth* (Young Geographers Series) Oxford 1989

McCracken, N *What Rubbish!* Oxford 1982

Ryan, F and Ray, S *Green Hints* Green Press 1990

Spurgeon, R *Ecology: A Practical Introduction with Projects and Activities* (Science and Experiments Series) Usborne 1988

Suzuki, D *Looking at the Environment* Allen and Unwin 1989

General Resources

(See also comprehensive resource list at back of book)

Australian Conservation Foundation *Personal Action Guide* 1989

Department of Planning and Urban Growth *101 Ways to Keep Vic Fit* 1989 (available from 447 Collins Street, Melbourne)

Elkington, J and Hailes, J *The Green Consumer Guide* Penguin 1988

Lord, B *The Green Cleaner* ACF 1988

Lord, B (with Frank Ryan and Stephen Ray) *50 Easy Things we can do so save the Planet* ACF 1990

Myers, N *The Gaia Atlas of Planet Management — for today's caretakers of tomorrow's world* Pan 1985

For useful contacts, see general resource list, (p. 196)

Listening and Looking

Listening . . .

Close your eyes and listen to the sounds around you for a few minutes or until your teacher tells you to stop. Then, write down all the things that you think you heard in the box below.

Things I heard . . .

Share your ideas with a friend.

Looking . . .

Now, make a list of all the things that you can see from where you are sitting.

Things I can see . . .

Is it natural?

Sort the things that you listed out in the school yard into these groups.

Natural	Human-made	Not sure

My Earth Wheel

Name_____

Date_____

Use words and pictures to fill in the four sections of this circle.

Things on earth that are abundant.

Things on earth that are scarce.

Ways we harm the environment.

Ways we help the environment.

Making Earth concept maps

Read through all the words on this sheet. If there are any that you're not sure about, talk to a friend about them.

Cut out all the words and then arrange them on a page in a way that makes sense to you.

Draw lines and arrows between the words that you think connect to each other in some way. You can draw as many lines and arrows as you like.

Write on the lines so that you can explain why the words connect to each other.

You can add words if you think you need to.

When you have finished your map, show it to a friend. He/she should be able to read sentences along parts of your map.

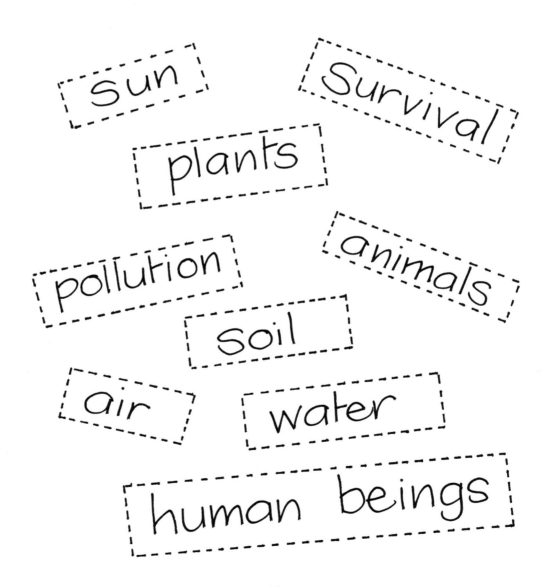

Role-play article

Grickle Grass Times.   Saturday 10th November 2000 $10.00

NEW THNEED FACTORY PROPOSED FOR GRICKLE-GRASS LAND!

In a shock statement from the local council today, residents of Grickle-Grass were told of a proposal to build a new Thneed factory. Mr G.D. Once-ler, a nephew of the late Mr Once-ler (who built the original factory many years ago) has presented plans to the council for a new factory that he says will provide the town with a lot of money and employment.

In an interview with the press today Mr Once-ler said: "The trufulla trees have all grown back now. In fact there are more than there were before! I know my uncle did things badly but I am not going to repeat his mistakes. Besides, I think this tired old town could do with a bit of money and Thneeds are as popular as ever!"

A spokesperson for the local conservation groups, Mr Lorax, disagreed. "I can't believe that this is happening again!" he exclaimed. "This man says that the factory will be cleaner but I don't see how. We have just got all the swommee-swans back in the lakes and now the water might be polluted all over again. I will fight this proposal head-on!"

A public meeting will be held in the town hall on Monday to discuss the proposed new factory.

Role-play cards

Mr G D Once-ler
You are the nephew of the Once-ler who built the original Thneed factory in the town. You want to build another factory because you know that Thneeds are still very popular. They sell for a very high price in shops and people are asking for more to be made. You think that it is important for more people to have jobs and you know that the factory will provide some.

Mr Lorax
You have been through all this before and you are ready to fight again. You do not think that the factory should be built because you have seen what it can do to the land, air, water and the birds and animals.

Mrs Barbaloot
You are worried that a factory for Thneeds will destroy your home. You need trufulla trees for food and shelter.

Miss O Funsler
You have been unemployed for a long time and you find it difficult to care for your two children. The factory would be good for you because it would give you a job.

Councillor
You are the chairperson, the organiser of the meeting. You need to make sure that everyone gets a fair say. At the end of the meeting you hope that you will all come up with a decision or some ideas to try out. You are not really sure what you think about the factory. Your main job is to keep order during the meeting.

What can I do?

List 3 things in each box that you could do to help look after the natural environment.

To help look after our soil I can:

1._____
2._____
3._____

To help look after our water I can:

1._____
2._____
3._____

To help look after animals I can:

1._____
2._____
3._____

To help look after plants I can:

1._____
2._____
3._____

To help look after the air I can:

1._____
2._____
3._____

My pledge to the Earth

My pledge to the Earth

I,_____

of_____

_____

promise to do the following three things to help look after Earth's
resources:

1._____

2._____

3._____

Signed_____

Witness_____

Date_____

Our pledge to the Earth

Our pledge to the Earth

*We,*_____*(Class),*

*of*_____*(School)*

    promise to do the following three things to help look after Earth's resources:

*1.*_____

*2.*_____

*3.*_____

*Signed*_____

Class representatives

*Date*_____

A World of their Own

An integrated unit of work about rainforests

Rationale

Rainforests have been described as the lungs of the Earth. They play an important part in regulating the Earth's climate through their position in the oxygen, carbon and water cycles. They are a rich source of biodiversity amongst living things, being home to almost half of the Earth's plant and animal species! Rainforests provide humans with many important raw materials for medicines, foods and other products.

The Earth's rainforests are diminishing at an alarming rate — almost 50% have already been destroyed and the destruction continues. The growth in population, technology, atmospheric pollution, poverty, unequal land distribution and pressure for timber, contribute to this ongoing and often unchecked destruction.

Many of the students we teach will never see a rainforest, they will never have direct contact with one of the most important natural environments on the Earth. A unit like this aims to take them there as best we can and to develop a respect and understanding for this essential ecosystem. A study of the rainforest is a study of a microcosm of the Earth from which students can learn a great deal.

Rainforests are ancient and delicate places. They are an important key to our understanding of life on Earth and yet so much about them is still to be discovered.

Contents

The list below is a summary of the activities that you will find in this unit. It is not suggested that you do them all but that you select some activities from under each major heading to suit your purposes.

Rainforest

The forest drips and glows with green
The tree frog croaks his far-off song
His voice is stillness, moss and rain
drunk from the forest ages long

We cannot understand that call
Unless we move into his dream
Where all is one and one is all
and frog and python are the same.

— from Judith Wright, *Phantom Dwelling*, 1985

About this Unit

This unit is designed to engage students in research and discovery and to introduce them to some of the most interesting and important places on the Earth. As a topic, it leads to the exploration of many key ecological concepts and demonstrates interesting characteristics of the relationship that humans have with their environment.

The unit takes students beyond their immediate environment and encourages them to appreciate another. In this way, it is an important part in educating them about the environment. We need to understand and respect environments — even those we may never see — for they all have an impact and effect on our lives.

Through research and role-play, students will also explore the nature of conflict and will gain an insight into the many complexities that environmental issues raise.

Understandings

- Rainforests are one of the most important ecosystems on Earth.
- Rainforests are a rich source of biodiversity containing much of the world's flora and fauna species.
- Humans use rainforests for many things. Many of these uses have had adverse effects on the rainforest.
- Many of the Earth's rainforests have already been cleared and they continue to be cleared at a rapid rate.
- Conflict has arisen over the fate of the Earth's remaining rainforests.
- Rainforests have characteristics that make them unique.
- There are things that we can do as individuals to help conserve rainforests.

Key concepts

Ecosystem   Diversity
Conservation   Cause and effect
Conflict   Wilderness

Skills

Predicting and imagining
Presenting an argument
Clarifying values
Decision making
Taking action
Classifying
Problem solving
Researching
Reporting

"A WORLD OF THEIR OWN" — SAMPLE UNIT PLANNER

Phase	Week	Session 1	Session 2	Session 3	Session 4	Session 5	Ongoing Activities	Comments:
Tuning In & Preparing to Find Out	Week 1	TUNING IN • Video "Where the Forest Meets the Sea" • Memory Game	• Special Places in Australia	• Mini Rainforest (groups & mural)	PREPARING TO FIND OUT • What is a rainforest?	Using trees BLM 1	Begin word lists using language generated so far. Add to mural.	
Finding Out	Week 2	FINDING OUT • Video – Earth First	• Const. Sharing notes and responses.	Art • Setting classroom up as a rainforest	• Setting classroom up as a rainforest.	• Setting classroom up as a rainforest.	Letter writing to organisations	
Sorting Out	Week 3	Drama – • Role-play activity BLM2	• Role play activity BLM2	Language • Written dialogue about drama activity	• Retrieval Chart – rainforest animals BLM3+4	• Cinquain Poetry	Reading factual texts.	
Going Further	Week 4	• Food chains based on chart	Music • a day in the life of the rainforest	• A day in the life of the rainforest – performance	Maths • Revisit video Maths facts	• Visual representation of statistics	Monitoring "mini rainforest"	
Making Connections	Week 5	Research – • Group research begins BLM5	Research – • Group research	Research – • Group research Presentations	GOING FURTHER • Rotating activities – Songs	Story Map	Rotating activities available in room.	
Taking Action	Week 6	• Conflict Matrix BLM6	MAKING CONNECTIONS • Futures wheels	TAKING ACTION • Information Brochures	• Information Brochures	Reflecting on unit		

Tuning in

The activities suggested here are designed simply to get students engaged in thinking about the topic. They are designed to sensitise and motivate students . . . to get the ball rolling.

One special place: the Daintree rainforest

Show the students the animated video of Jeannie Baker's *Where the Forest Meets the Sea* (Film Australia, 1988, 10 minutes). This video is an excellent way to set the tone for the unit. It engages students in the beauty and wonder of an ancient rainforest and provides them with some visual information about rainforests. The conservation message in the video is clear and may spark some initial discussion about issues that will be re-visited in more depth during the unit.

I went to the rainforest and I saw . . .

A fun, follow-up to the video is a variation on the game 'I went shopping'. Instead, students say 'I went to the rainforest and I saw . . . ' They recall what they saw in the video and must remember all previous items offered by others.

At the end of the game, having gone around the whole grade, make a list of all the things that were seen. A mural of these could be made using the collage technique seen in the film.

Special Places

Ask students to close their eyes and to think about a special, outdoor place that they like being in or have been to. They may have been somewhere on a holiday or their special place might be somewhere close to home. Ask them these questions:

What is it called?
Think about the sort of environment that your special place is. Is it flat? hilly? dark? sunny?
What does it smell like? What noises can you hear?

In small groups, students share their special places with each other.

Display a map of Australia or your state. Mark the 'special places' using name tags and blu-tack. Discuss the most popular places using the questions below:

- Why do we go there?
- What type of environments do we visit?
- How do they make us feel?

Using a map of Australia, show students the areas such as Northern Queensland in which tropical rainforests are to be found. Ask them what sort of environment they think would be here. Brainstorm ideas.

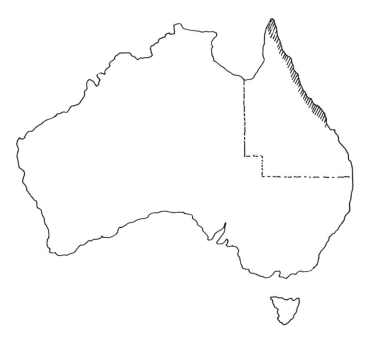

A mini rainforest

This is set up and observed throughout the course of the unit. A daily observation sheet is filled out by various students.

Using a fish tank, students can create an environment similar to that of a tropical rainforest in the classroom!

- Place a layer of gravel at the bottom of the fish tank.
- Cover with a layer of compost and leaf litter.
- Add a variety of plants that will grow at different levels (e.g. mosses, ferns, creepers).
- Cover the terrarium and watch the way the water recycles between compost, air, plant and tank.
- Spray the inside of the terrarium lightly with water about once a week.
- Watch your mini-rainforest and see what happens!

N.B. This is a good opportunity to construct a procedural text: 'How to make your own mini rainforest'

Preparing to find out

These activities are designed with three main aims:

1. To give you some insight into what the students already know about the topic and where their initial interests lie;

2. To help students focus clearly on what they already know and what they will try to find out.

(Some activities require the students to make decisions about the ways they will go about gathering information);

3. To prepare the students for the experience to follow and to focus their investigations.

What is a rainforest?

Have some posters of rainforest around the room. There are some beautiful posters available from environment centres and conservation organisations throughout Australia (see resource list near the end of the unit).

In groups, ask students to brainstorm the question: What is a rainforest? In what ways do you think they are different from other forests? Ask them to record their ideas on a chart.

At this stage accept all ideas — students will have a chance to modify them throughout the unit. Leave these charts up around the room for students to return to when they have more information.

> A rainforest is like a jungle (Peter)
>
> It rains a lot in rainforests (Rachel)
>
> I think there are a lot of reptiles in rainforests. (Miroslav)

How do we use forests?

Look around the room. Ask students what things in the classroom they think have been made from wood. Do the same at home. Keep a list in the classroom that can be added to throughout the unit. Ask students about the other ways we use trees. Use the chart on BLM 1 (p. 81).

How is the tree used?	Does it satisfy a need or a want?	What could be used instead?
For building houses	need (shelter)	bricks
For pencils	want	pens
For desks	want	nothing, I think wood is best for this.

What do we want to know about rainforests?

Ask students to think of one thing they would like to know about rainforests. Individuals write their questions out on cards.

Categorise the cards as a grade. Which questions go together? Display the questions with the students' names on each.

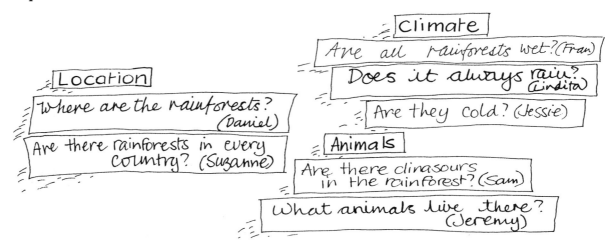

How will we find out?

Students make a list of ways in which they could find out more about rainforests: discuss the most appropriate actions. Students decide which things are feasible for the class to do and consider the type of information they will get from these various sources.

Suggest that students begin by writing to appropriate organisations seeking information. Model a letter with the whole class first, in the style of a wall story. Students use the model to write their own letters.

Relevant national and international organisations are listed in the resource section of this unit. State organisations can be found by contacting your local department of conservation or an environment centre. This would be a useful exercise for students. It is important that information is gathered from a broad range of sources. Write to state timber industry authorities, government departments, and conservation groups.

Finding out

This experience is designed to give students the opportunity to gather new information about the topic.

Excursions

A *visit to a rainforest* would obviously be a valuable shared experience for this unit. By contacting your state department of conservation or local tourist authority, find out whether there are any accessible areas of rainforest for you to visit. This will of course depend on where your school is situated and the resources available to you.

Alternatively, you may find an area of your nearest capital city's botanical gardens or zoological gardens that is planted out to model a rainforest. Many large botanical gardens have education officers who will design activities for school groups based on the topic you are studying.

If you do decide to use this direct experience it is wise to involve students in some specific activities such as:

- playing a variety of environmental outdoor games (available from your state's Gould League Centre) or
- having a gardener talk to you about the rainforest plants.

Selected videos and films

There are a number of superb videos about rainforests that are suitable for upper primary students. In fact, an audio-visual resource may provide students with more information to process than an unguided visit to a rainforest. Perhaps you could do both! Below are focus questions for watching the video :

- What do you find out about rainforests?
- Why is there such conflict over rainforests?

A highly recommended video that is widely available is *Earth First*, narrated by Jack Thompson, (Joymar Productions 1986). This video provides an excellent introduction to Australia's rainforests. As well as giving information about what a rainforest is, it examines a number of conflicts that have occurred over the logging of particular rainforests such as Terrania Creek and the Daintree. When using the video with students, be selective. It is too much all at once! Use only portions of it and stop to reflect on and talk about what you have seen. It may be wise to watch it over two or three sittings. (See resources at the end of the unit for other suggested videos and films.)

Many rainforest action groups will send out a speaker to schools on request. Often, their talks are accompanied by slides or videos. Always request that the talk focuses both on rainforests in general as well as the conflict of interest that occurs over their use. Similarly, speakers from your state's timber industry may available to speak to school groups.

It is important that students have opportunities to gather information from a wide range of resources.

Sorting out

At this stage, a variety of activities is suggested across a range of curriculum areas. Students will process information they have gathered and present it in a number of different ways. They may also begin to draw some conclusions about what it is they have learned.

As an introductory activity, ask students to collate their responses to the two focus questions in the video activity above. Each student then shares their ideas with two others and the three come up with a common list. Two groups, each of three members, merge and create a final list common to the six members. (This strategy is called a 1–3-6 consensus strategy. Of course the number in each group should be varied if the total number in the class is not divisible by three!)

Revisiting our original ideas

Re-visit the ideas recorded in 'What is a rainforest?' above. Address these questions:

● Is there anything we want to change or add?
● Have any of your questions been answered?
● Do we have new questions to ask?

Art

Adding to the mural

The students have already used collage to represent some of their initial ideas about rainforests. A small group may want to add to the mural some of the things that they saw on the video or during a visit to a rainforest.

From classroom to rainforest

As a way of further representing the ideas from the shared experience, students can make the classroom into a rainforest! Use the following steps to develop this activity:

Step 1 — What should be included?

Announce that the class is going to turn the room into a rainforest. Ask students what they think should be represented in the rainforest model. Consider for example, the canopy, the middle layer, the forest floor, vines, darkness, various rainforest animals and buttresses.

Step 2 — Planning

Tell students, 'In small groups I'd like you to make a plan for the way we could best turn our room into a rainforest. Remember that we still have to work here and move around! Think about the art materials that we have got and the time available to us. Label your plan so that others can understand it.'

Step 3 — Group work

Display the plans and select from the range of ideas those that are achievable. Each group then chooses (or is designated) one area to work on. Have some texts available for any research that may be required. Nominate students to gather the necessary materials. Again, encourage them to plan their task and to allocate roles.

Step 4 — Creating

Spend an afternoon creating the rainforest room. Students must justify what goes where. For example, 'This frog is a tree dweller.'

Step 5 — The finishing touches

As a language/handwriting activity, students write statements for various parts of the display to inform others about the rainforest.

Invite other students into your rainforest. Encourage students to add to the various displays during their free time.

Portraying conflict

A less ambitious project is to ask the students to depict, through art, some of the conflicts that they found out about from the video. They may choose a particular issue to focus on or represent the notion of conflict in the rainforest generally.

Again this art work can be followed up with a labelling activity to explain the piece to others.

Drama

The conservation of rainforests remains an issue that has led to a number of conflicts between those who want to alter the environment in some way and those who want to conserve it. Some of these issues are discussed on the *Earth First* video. They are also more simply portrayed in Jeannie Baker's *Where the Forest Meets the Sea*.

For this drama activity, one particular issue is used to explore the various interests and ideas that can lead to conflict. This issue centres around the rainforest in far North Queensland and, in particular, the conflict that began during the eighties over the road that has been constructed between Bloomfield and Cape Tribulation, through a section of the rainforest. This issue is a good example of the conflict of interests that can occur over environmental decisions. It is not a simple case but one in which there are a range of views and opinions. The case has also been selected for this unit because of students' increasing knowledge and interest in the area through books like *Where the Forest Meets the Sea* (see pages 82 & 83 for the scenario and role cards).

The *Earth First* video outlines the conflict. Further information about the issue is available from the Australian Conservation Foundation, rainforest action groups and the timber industry. It is wise to get a range of material that gives students a variety of views and information. (See address list in list of resources at end of unit.)

It is most likely that the issue will be explored by the material that has been sent to the students. You can make specific requests for copies of relevant articles about the issue from the Australian Conservation Foundation. A number of the resources listed at the end of the unit also deal well with the issue.

Role-Play — the Daintree blockade

Step 1
Discuss the information and articles that you have already received about the issue to ensure that students have an understanding of the basic areas of conflict.

Step 2
Present them with the scenario outlined on BLM 2 (page 82).

Step 3
Number students off from 1–5. Each number corresponds to a character outlined on the scenario sheet.

Step 4
Students move into support groups (all students with the same number) to discuss their roles. In these groups they should establish what sort of person they are, what they believe about the issue, arguments to support their ideas etc. They may choose to visit other groups during this time to enlist support or lobby. Encourage students to record the ideas they get from their support group to use when they join the public meeting. The support groups may spend some time organising simple props or costumes for themselves to help them assume their role. Examples of props for each character:

- Ms I. Nowall — a pair of glasses
- Mr G. Reenie — a conservation badge
- Mr G. Imepoor — a shop apron
- Johnny Greenwood — fishing accessories
- Mr S. Goldsworthy — a tie
- Chairperson — a clipboard

Step 5
Once students have been given sufficient time to develop their role in a group, you (the local newspaper editor or town mayor) announce that the public meetings are about to begin. Call the meetings to order. Students assemble in their meeting groups where there will be one representative of each character.

Step 6
The instructions for the meeting should be that groups are to come up with some *recommendations* in the time given that may help resolve the issue.

Each group should appoint a chairperson to make sure that people get a fair hearing and to report back at the end of the meeting.

Step 7
When the meetings are finished, ask students to reform their support groups. This is a debriefing time. Discuss the following questions:

- How did you feel in the meeting?
- What was easy for you?
- What was difficult?
- What were the similarities and differences in your experiences?
- What would you do differently next time?

Share some of these observations as a whole class. Discuss together the outcome of the meetings as well as the way individual participants felt during the meeting. This debriefing time is very important as it assists students in clarifying their understandings of both the issue and the nature of conflict and resolution.

Interviews
Should this role-play appear too ambitious for your students, an alternative is to use the character cards in pairs and conduct mock TV interviews with characters about the issue.

Language

Written dialogue

An effective follow-up to the drama activity is to ask students to work in pairs or small groups and actually write down the dialogue that occurred in the meetings. They can do this in the form of a script with various characters putting forward their point of view.

Poetry

As an opportunity to explore a different form of writing, students could use the information presented in the video and related literature to develop some of their own poetry about rainforests.

Provide students with a structure for their writing, such as the one below:

Cinquain poem
1. Title — one word (subject)

2. Two words that describe subject

3. Three words that describe the activity of the subject

4. Descriptive phrase (four words)

5. Synonym for title

(Of course, strictly speaking, a cinquain poem has lines of two, four, six, eight and two syllables, but you may not wish to be that prescriptive.)

Here is an example of one student's work:

> Vine
> Soft, tangled
> Twisting, stretching, growing
> Wrapping around the trees
> String

Students nominate one part of the rainforest or a rainforest plant or animal (perhaps from the class topic list generated through the theme) and use that word to develop a poem.

Share poetry about rainforests with students. One example is Judith Wright's *Rainforest*. Although the language may appear complex, students will sense the atmosphere she is trying to create through her choice of words. Talk with students about what they think she is trying to say and about the way she uses language to take you to the rainforest.

Retrieval charts

Revisit *Where the Forest Meets the Sea* and any other literature on rainforest animals. Develop a class retrieval chart based on the rainforest animals seen in the book or on the video and those that the students have found out about during the unit so far.

Name	Appearance	Characteristics	Habitat	Food	Threats	Protective Devices
Green-tree Snake	Bright green, long	Rests in special coiled position	Trees	Bats, mice	-Logging -Some birds -People -Cyclones	-Camouflage in trees

A class chart could be developed after individuals or small groups have completed their own chart using BLMs 3 and 4. Students work on various groups of animals, e.g. birds, insects, mammals, reptiles, amphibians. These could then be transferred to the large class chart or could also be constructed as a computer data-base using programs such as *Apple Works*.

The chart could also be used to record information about rainforest plants.

After compiling the list, ask students to note any patterns they see. Ask questions like these:

- What can we say about the threats to rainforest animals and plants?
- Which animals and plants appear to be most threatened? Why?
- What can we say about the protective devices used by rainforests animals and plants?
- What other patterns do you notice from our chart?

Students keep adding to the list as they find out about rainforest animals.

Having completed the retrieval chart, ask students to try to put some animals into a food chain. Add plants to the food chain using BLM 3 (on page 84). An example can be found below:

What would happen to your food chain when the rainforest is logged? (a list of rainforest animals and plants is provided (BLM p. 84).

The webbing game

The rainforest food chain can be physically demonstrated by playing the 'webbing game'. BLM 4 will assist here. One student becomes the sun and holds a ball of wool or string. Teacher asks 'What does the sun give energy to?' (Answer: plants.) Some students volunteer to be plants and attach themselves to the string as it unravels further. 'Which animals might eat these plants?' Some animals such as insects attach themselves and so on.

The web becomes complicated as animals will have a variety of dependent relationships within it. Once a 'web' has been made, tug a student who is a tree and explain that she has just been chopped down. Any student connected with that tree must bob down too and so on, until all the links in the chain are broken.

Text analysis and writing reports

Show students some examples of literature that deals with topics in a report style. Some suggestions follow:

- Howes, J. *Five Trees* Macmillan 1988
- Young, A. and Heinrich, H *Remnants of Green* Kangaroo Press 1989
- Woolley, M. and Pigdon, K. *Earthworms* Macmillan 1989

Discuss these questions with the students to assist them in understanding the construction of factual texts:

- What do you think the author needed to know about the topic to write this book?
- How do you think the author gathered the information?
- How has the author organised the information? (Consider, for example, appearance, habitat, characteristics, threats.)
- How has the author tried to make the information clear and interesting to the reader?

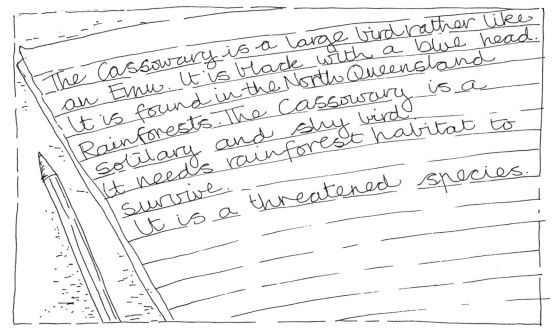

The Cassowary is a large bird rather like an Emu. It is black with a blue head. It is found in the North Queensland Rainforests. The Cassowary is a solitary and shy bird. It needs rainforest habitat to survive. It is a threatened species.

Students use this model and the data charts they have constructed to develop their own reports on one animal or plant of the rainforest. Publish the reports in a class book. The text of the reports may also be used as the basis of cloze activities.

Wilderness quotation

'Wilderness should be there for people all around Australia, it should be there for everybody around the world. It should be there for the inhabitants of that wilderness, our fellow creatures on this planet who don't get a vote ... if we don't have the humility to consider our fellow creatures in nature, be they trees, be they living in the trees or on the forest floor, there is no hope for us as part of the realm of nature.'

Dr Bob Brown in Borschumann, G. *Greater Daintree*, ACF, 1984, p. 26.

Discuss this quotation using the following questions:

- What is Dr Brown saying?
- How does he use language to try to convince you?
- Do you agree with him? Why? Why not?
- Are people the dominant species? Why?
- Who should be in control?

Music

Both the *Where the Forest Meets the Sea* and the *Earth First* videos are visually arresting. They are made even more powerful by the sound track that accompanies them.

One way of developing students' sensitivity towards the rainforest is to encourage them to make their own sound-track for a series of visual images of the forest.

An image and sound show

Sets of slides that depict beautiful rainforest scenes are available from libraries, conservation departments, rainforest action groups, zoo education services and the Gould League.

Show students a portion of the video again and ask them to listen to the sounds that are used to accompany the images. What instruments can you hear? Why do you think they have been chosen? What songs are used? Why? How effective are they?

Show students a slide set of the rainforest. Ask them to listen 'in their heads' to the sort of music that could accompany the slides.

Give one or two slides to pairs or trios of students. Their task is to create the 'backing track' to that particular scene using instruments (percussion would be fine), recorded music, voices etc. They may need access to a music room to do this. When all groups have their piece ready, they perform an 'image and sound show'. Show all the slides and ask each group to provide the appropriate accompaniment. Invite another class or parents to hear and watch your show.

Should you have difficulty obtaining your slides, groups could create a poster of the rainforest or use those around the room and then compose the appropriate backing music.

A day in the life of a rainforest

Another way to use music to develop students' appreciation of the rainforest is to provide groups with a different part of the day to depict using voice and percussion instruments. They may choose from the times and events below:

- Daybreak in the rainforest
- A morning downpour
- Afternoon heat
- Evening falling
- Night in the rainforest

First discuss with students what they think would happen in the rainforest at these different times. For an added contrast ask the same groups to devise sounds for the same time of day in a different environment, such as the city.

Musical poetry

Students could develop some simple musical background for their cinquain rainforest poems. Each line is an effective basis for some sort of sound effect.

Maths

The topic of rainforests lends itself particularly well to explorations of statistics and the concepts of time and area. The following activities are designed to develop students' understanding of rainforests through mathematical investigations. They follow the video particularly well and are designed to give a new perspective to processing the shared experience.

Facts and Figures

Revisit the introduction to the *Earth First* video. Ask students to make a note of all the 'mathematical' information they receive. Students may select one fact that interests them and try to represent that idea visually. For example, many of the statistics on forest depletion could be represented by a graph.

Time-line

Use the information below about the formation of rainforests to develop a giant time-line. Illustrations could be made to accompany the timeline.

The formation of rainforests
130 million years ago
Australia was part of 'Gondwanaland', a huge land mass including Africa, India, South America, Antarctica, New Zealand and New Caledonia. The first flowering plants appeared at this time.

20 million years ago
Gondwanaland began to separate.

80 million years ago
By now, Africa, South America, and India had broken away, as had New Zealand and New Caledonia.

50 million years ago
Australia broke away from Antarctica and drifted northward. Many species of plant and animal were now unique to that land mass because it was isolated.

35 million years ago
As the climate became drier, new plants began to emerge, such as eucalyptus, banksia and grevillea. The rainforest areas were reduced in size and were located in the wetter parts of the continent.

15 million years ago
New plant and animal species appeared when Australia collided with the Asian Plate.

2 to 10 million years ago
Rainforests were reduced even further during the glacial period.

1800s to present
European settlement saw the clearing of more than half the remaining rainforest.

Rainforests are remnants of the ancient time of Gondwanaland. They grow in places where the climate is similar to what it was 130 million years ago. Many of the plants found in rainforests are ancient relics of some of the very first flora.

Some problem solving activities

The statistics below could be presented simply as discussion starters or used as the basis for calculations and visual representation activities.

- Rainforest occupies about 20,000 square kilometres of Australia.
- This is about 0.3% of the country. Our rainforests would fit into a circle of about 70 km radius.

About 3/4 of our rainforest has been destroyed in the last 200 years. How much rainforest was there before white settlement? Can you show rainforest cover before and after white settlement?

- It is estimated that one 'football field' of rainforest is cleared every minute. How big is an average football field? (100m by 73m or 7300m^2 or 0.73 hectares)

Use your calculator to find out how much is cleared every hour, every day, every week? Can you show this information on a graph?
What would speed up the depletion of rainforests? What would slow it down?
In Australia, our rainforests are distributed as follows:

- Queensland 54.9%
- Tasmania 30.6%
- New South Wales 11.2%
- Victoria 0.6%
- Northern Territory 1.7%
- Western Australia <0.1%

Find out where the rainforest areas are in each state. Can you show the different areas of rainforest in each state on a map? Can you find out what the original percentage of our total rainforest cover was for each state? Why has this changed?
Most information on rainforests includes statistics such as the above. A good source of statistics is the Australian Heritage Commission (see

reference list). In order for students to understand the significance of some of these figures, it is useful for them to represent the statistics visually in some way.

One interesting exercise is for the students simply to record all the statistics they find on one particular issue (e.g. total yearly forest loss). The statistics often vary markedly and generate some very interesting discussion about the nature of 'numerical' information such as this. Discuss the source that the statistics come from and their intended purpose and audience. What other factors need to be taken into account when we examine the graphs we have made? What don't they show?

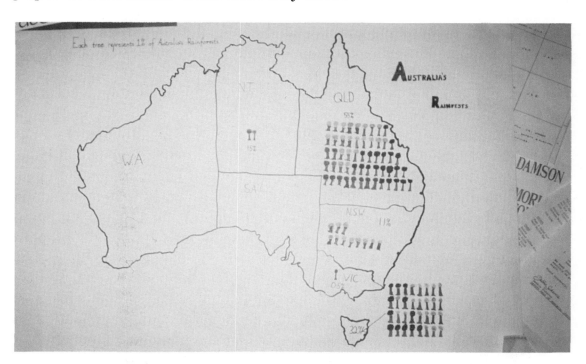

Going further

These activities are designed to challenge and extend students' understandings about the topic.

Research

By this stage in the unit, students will have received information that they sent away for, and you will have gathered a class collection of resources on rainforests. This is an opportune time for students to be engaged in some sort of independent research, either on their own or with a small groups.

Ideas for independent research are listed below. Ideally, however, the ideas should be generated by the students and arise from work done so far in the unit.

(This is a good time to revisit original statements and questions about the topic. Students may discover that some of their questions are yet to be answered and this may form the basis for their own project.)

Students may use the research planning pro forma provided in BLM 5 (page 86) in order to investigate the topics suggested below:

● Indigenous People and the Rainforest
   Find out about a group of people who live in the rainforest. How do they manage the rainforest without altering its ecology?

● Gourmet Delights
   Find out about the food that we get from the rainforest.

● Green Pharmacy
   Find out about the medicines that originate in the rainforest

● Climate
   What is the temperature and rainfall in a rainforest? Does it change much? Why? In what ways does the climate differ in different types of rainforests.

● Green Factory
   Find out about the products that come from rainforests and about how they are used (e.g. rubber and timber). Which countries produce them? Which countries buy them?

Rotating activities

Select from below a range of related experiences to fine-tune understandings. These could be set up in the room for a week and students visit them in alloted times. They may do all the activities or simply attend the ones that they are interested in.

Songs

Have some songs about rainforests and the environment on tape, such as:

- *If a Tree Falls in the Forest* Bruce Cockburn (Big Circumstance)
- *Fragile* Sting (Nothing Like the Sun)
- *Dream World* Midnight Oil (Diesel and Dust)
- *Rip, Rip, Wood Chip* John Williamson
- *Leave that Tree Alone* (Gould League Environmental Songs tape)
- *Universe's Daughter* Fay White; from Soil Ain't Dirt Landcare songs, Department of Conservation and Environment, Victoria.

Compare the songs. Are they all saying the same thing? What did the writers feel? How do they make you feel? Who do you think would like the song? Who would not like the song? Which song do you like best? Why? Which song do you like least? Why?

These songs could be taped onto a listening post and be available for students to listen to in their own time.

Books

Have some picture story books available for students to examine. They could then choose one book as the basis for a literature activity (see resource page at end of unit). Below are some suggested activities:

- Story map

  Students illustrate scenes from a story showing the sequence of events.

- Book report

  Students prepare a review of the story including a summary of they main events, special features of the text and illustrations and their opinion of the book.

- Character profile

  Students select one character from the story to explore in detail. They prepare a personal profile of that character using the information in the book and make any additions they think appropriate.

Newspaper articles

Provide a range of newspaper articles about rainforests, without their headlines (Copies of these are available from the Heritage Commission and from the Australian Conservation Foundation.) Students devise a headline for each. Alternatively, make the headlines available. Students write the accompanying report, then compare it to the original.

Audio-tapes

Audio-tapes about rainforests (and other environmental issues) are available through the Australian Broadcasting Corporation. Some are a little complex but small sections could be easily comprehended and are an excellent resource for a school.

Conflict matrix — threats to the rainforest

Students use BLM 6 and work in pairs to decide which uses of rainforest might cause a conflict of interest. This could then be a source of discussion and debate.

Making connections

At this stage, students will be drawing conclusions about what they have learnt. This is an important time for you to evaluate the success of the unit and the needs and achievements of individuals. This is where students 'put it all together'.

Revising and revisiting

Revisit original ideas about what makes a rainforest a rainforest.

Is there anything students wish to add or change?

Revisit our questions about rainforests. Each student can select a question for which they can provide an answer. Write the answer on a strip of card and display.

Futures wheels

This exercise is similar to concept mapping but focussed more on the idea of cause and effect. The exercise asks students to demonstrate their understandings about the delicate nature of the rainforest. The wheel begins with a central cause then radiates out showing direct and indirect consequences (see opposite).

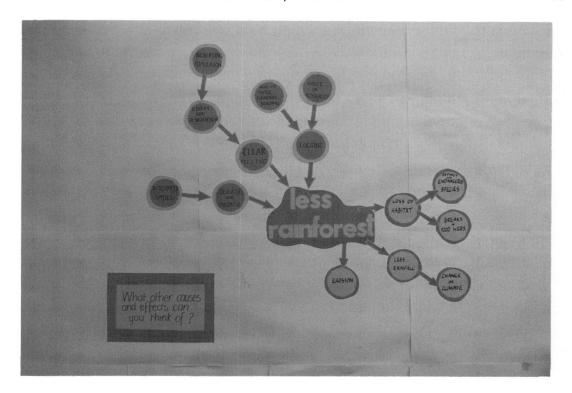

Students may think up their own futures wheels for rainforests — they could provide both a positive and negative alternative.

Taking action

This is a very important element of both the inquiry process and of environmental education. It is essential that students be given opportunities to act upon what they have learnt.

Spend some time reflecting on what has been learnt so far. Students may wish to add to their rainforest room or change some of the statements that they have on display.

Information brochure

This is one way that students can engage in some sort of action for the rainforest and also demonstrates some of their understandings to you. Their task is to design an information brochure to encourage people to visit and look after rainforests. It may be an Australian rainforest or they may wish to promote a rainforest they have found out about elsewhere in the world.

Begin this activity by showing the students some tourist brochures or information leaflets designed for other special places — these can be obtained from the state tourist authority or various conservation groups. Analyse the way that brochures are presented and the different audiences they seem to be pitched at.

As a class, decide on what sort of information you will need in your rainforest brochures, such as:

- Information about *where* the rainforest is;
- Information about *what* a rainforest is and what *lives* there;
- Information about *how to get there*;
- Information about why rainforests are *special*;
- *Pictures* of the rainforests;
- *Maps*;
- *Rules* about the things that you can and cannot do in a rainforest.

A further challenge would be for students to identify particular audiences for their brochures — is the information intended for families, for bush walkers, for elderly people, for an overseas visitor, for others?

Upon completion, students send their brochures to someone to inform them about rainforests.

Letters
Write letters to appropriate groups to express concern for or interest in rainforests. (See resource list.)

Other activities
- Sponsor an animal at the zoo that comes from the rainforest.
- Reduce the amount of paper used, reuse and recycle it. (This is a way of looking after all forests.) Students can make a difference here and it is an easy activity to begin in the school. Reducing and reusing are the important things to do. Discuss ways that you could use less paper in your room. Discuss other things that students could do in their personal lives that would make as difference.
- Invite a speaker from a rainforest action group to speak to other grades in the school.
- Visit other grades and give talks on the rainforest. Use the slide and sound show to accompany talks.
- Keep an eye out for information in the paper about rainforests throughout the world. Compile a class scrapbook that can be taken home and discussed with families.

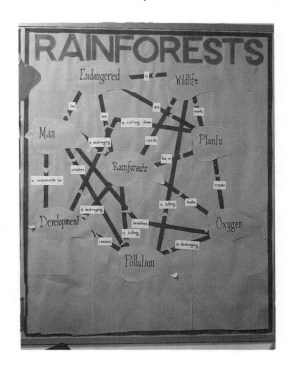

Resources

Children's literature

Baker, J. *Where the Forest Meets the Sea* Julia Macrae 1987

Banks, M. *Conserving Rainforests* (Conserving our World Series) Lothian 1991

Breidahl, H. *The Richest Forest* Macmillan 1987

Fisher, A. *A Tree with a Thousand Uses* Bowmar 1977

Greenwood, T. *V I P: Very Important Plant* Angus and Robertson 1971

Howes, J. *Five Trees* Macmillan 1987

Silverstein, Shel *The Giving Tree* Harper and Row 1964

Wheatley, N. *The Blooding* Viking Kestrel 1987

Young, A. and Heinrich, H. *Remnants of Green: A Rainforest Journey* Kangaroo Press 1989

Teaching resources

The Australian Heritage Commission has some very useful information about rainforests and world heritage areas in their kit, *Australia's Native Forests.* Write to GPO Box Canberra ACT 2601 (06) 271 2211

Mackness, B. *Mastering Rainforests* Dellasta 1989

Mackness, B. et al. *Cuscuses and Cassowaries* Ashton Scholastic 1987

Ministry of Education and Department of Conservation (Vic.), Forests and Lands *Trees and Forests — a resource kit for Schools* 1986 Melbourne

NSW National Parks and Wildlife Services have a good teacher's kit called *Aussie Trees Please* (1986) available from the NSW National Parks and Wildlife Service shop, Box N189 Grosvenor Street Post Office Sydney NSW 2000. Also relevant is their kit, *Why National Parks?*

Pugh, D. *Forests Activity Book* Rainforest Publishing Sydney 1987

General information on rainforests

Contact your local state department for environment (see general resource list)

ACF Habitat Education Supplement *Australia's Tropical Rainforests*, April 1987

Australian Conservation Foundation *Rainforest* ACF 1981

Australian Heritage Commission *Australia's Native Forests: An Information Kit.*

Caufield, C. *In the Rainforest* Picador 1985

Crome, Francis *Rainforests* Hodder and Stoughton 1982

Myers, N. *The Primary Source: Tropical Forests and Our Future* Norton and Co. 1984

Useful addresses

Australian Conservation Foundation
GPO Box 1875, Canberra, ACT
Australian Heritage Commission
GPO Box 1567 Canberra ACT
Australian National Parks and Wildlife Association.
GPO Box 636, Canberra, ACT 2601
(ANPWA has branches in each state)
East Gippsland Coalition
247 Flinders Lane
Melbourne, Vic 3000
Rainforest Action Group
PO Box 368 , Lismore, NSW 2480
Rainforest Information Centre
PO Box 368, Lismore, NSW 2480
Timber Development Association, NSW
PO Box 34, Strawberry Hills,
NSW 2012
Timber Promotion Council
932 Swanston Street
Carlton, Vic. 3054

Videos and films

Available through New South Wales and Victorian Departments of Education film and video libraries

Bellamy's Daintree: Where Reef Meets Rainforest video, 25 minutes. Australian Wilderness Society and Australian Conservation Foundation, 1987

Caroline and the Frog: An East Gippsland Story, Video, 23 minutes; Wilderness Society 1988

Give Trees a Chance (16 mm film, 11 minutes) Sydney Filmmaker's Co-op, 1980.

Jungle (*Living Planet* Series), David Attenborough (Available through the ABC)

Last Stands, 16 mm film, 45 min.; Island films, 1982

The Rainforest 16 mm film, 11 min.; Australian Educational Media, 1978

Where the Forest Meets the Sea, video, 10 min.; Film Australia, 1987

How do we use trees?

How is the tree used?	Does it satisfy a need or a want?	What could be used instead?

Public Meeting — Bloomfield Town Hall

Should the Bloomfield Road be closed?

A public meeting has been called to discuss the fate of the Bloomfield Road. Although the road has been open since 1984, there is still some conflict over its use. Some people think that the road has caused damage to the rainforest and the reef and that it should be closed so that the forest is allowed to grow over. They also feel that the road has not been a success and that it is poorly maintained. Other people feel that the road has brought increased tourism to the area and has made the lives of the residents of the town easier as they have better access to facilities.

There are still protesters at the entrance to the road who maintain that the road should be closed. They stop traffic and explain this to them before they begin their journey into the forest. They call their action a moral blockade.

The community has decided to try to reach a decision on the issue and will hold a meeting to discuss what has happened so far and to consider the future of the road.

The following representatives will be present at the meeting.

1. Ms I. Nowall — a teacher at the local primary school. She is for the road because she believes that the school has had better access to equipment and resources, more people come to visit the community, and more teachers are likely to want to work in the school if they feel they are less isolated. She is also concerned for the safety of children and wants to make the access easier for medical supplies and emergencies. She loves the forest but feels that it is important for the community that there is a road.

2. Ms G. Reenie — a conservationist who has been protesting against the road before it was built and now wants it to be closed. She is a science student at a Queensland university and has studied rainforests for a number of years. She has been arrested in previous conflicts over the rainforest. She is concerned that keeping the road open will continue to do damage to the nearby reef. She does not think that the road has been very successful.

3. Mr G. Imepoor — a shopkeeper who has always found it difficult to get supplies into the town. He has lived in the area all his life. Having the road through the rainforest has meant that it is much easier to get supplies and he has a better range of them. He has also found it much easier to do business out of town without having to make the day-trip around the cape. He has children that attend the local school.

4. Johnny Greenwood — a 9-year-old who moved to the area only a few years ago with his family. He has spent hours exploring the rainforest and the reef. His favourite pastime is fishing on the reef with his mum, then cooking the fish afterwards. He doesn't think the road is such a good idea and wants to have his say at the meeting.

5. Mr S. Goldworthy — a real estate agent who is in the business of selling land. He thinks the road is a good thing because it means that more people have access to the area and will be more likely to buy property. He thinks that this is, in fact, a good thing for the forest because if more people built their houses there, they would see how special it was and that we should not destroy it.

6. Chairperson — a member of the local council whose role it is to ensure that the meeting runs smoothly and that everyone gets to have a say. He/she is also hoping that the meeting will come up with some ideas and recommendations that can be taken back to the council. As far as a personal opinion about the road goes . . . he/she has not really decided yet.

Plants and animals found in the rainforests of northern Queensland

This is just a tiny sample of the plants and animals that have been discovered in the tropical rainforests of northern Queensland. **Many of these animals and plants are found nowhere else and rely on the rainforest environment for their survival and protection.**

cassowary

Cairns birdwing butterfly

puff-breasted paradise kingfisher

Boyds forest dragon lizard

white lemuroid possum

green tree frog

toothbilled cat bird

white-tailed kingfisher

Ulysses butterfly

golden orb weaver spider

noisy pitta bird

land snail

Victoria rifle bird

satin bower bird

brush turkey

wompoo pigeon

musk rat kangaroo

Lumholtz tree kangaroo

fruit bat

blossom bat

amethystene python

common green treesnake

pink-tongued lizard

leaf-tailed gecko

chameleon gecko

Eastern water dragon

red-eyed tree frog

giant tree frog

Herbert River ring-tailed possum

green ant

Jezebel butterfly

prickly forest skink

curtain fig tree

fan palm

stilt-rooted tree

tree fern

cycad

pandanus

lawyer vine

staghorn fern

strangler fig

bracket funghi

stinging tree

Most rainforest animal species are invertebrates like insects and worms. *Many have yet to be discovered — yet they play an important part in the food web.*

Data collection—animals

Rainforests are special places because they are home to many of the Earth's species of plants and animals. Rainforests have a fantastic range of rare and beautiful animals.

Team up with a friend and fill this chart in together. Choose *one group* of animals to work on (birds, reptiles, insects, amphibians, mammals). Use the information you have gathered about rainforest animals. You may also need to use some reference books. Try to make some guesses before you check in a book or other source of information.

Name					
Appearance					
Characteristics					
Habitat					
Food					
Threats					
Protection					

A World of their Own

Planning our investigation
A Research Contract

This contract sheet is designed to help you plan your mini-project and work out the things each person in your group will do. It is important that you agree on your research and that you plan something you think you will be able to get done in time. When you have completed the sheet, take it to your teacher to discuss and then sign the contract.

Names of people in research group _____

_____

_____

_____

_____

Topic _____

_____

Things we would like to find out (list questions) _____

_____

_____

_____

_____

Ways we will gather information (list books, places, people etc.) _____

_____

_____

_____

_____

Who will do what? _____

_____

_____

_____

_____

How will we present the information? _____

_____

Agreed deadline _____

Signatures (after discussion with your teacher) _____

_____

_____

_____

Conflict matrix — threats to the rainforest

This table is called a matrix. You use it in the same way that you find places on a road map. On the edges of the matrix are a list of things that rainforests are used for and conditions or characteristics of rainforests.

You need to work out which things *conflict* with each other and which things don't, that is, ways in which there can be a conflict between the rainforest itself and the ways it is used.

Use a √ if you think the two things go together.
Use a ○ if you think that one thing *could* go with another.
Use a × if you think that the two things definitely *don't* go together.
(Some examples have been done for you).

	Place of special interest to scientists	A home for many different types of plants and animals	Wilderness	National park	Water catchment (stores water that can be used for drinking)	Logging for wood and paper	Clearing for housing	Picnics	Bushwalking	Fishing	Trail-bike riding	Motor rallies
Place of special interest to scientists												
A home for many different types of plants and animals												
Wilderness												
National park												
Water catchment (stores water that can be used for drinking)												
Logging for wood and paper												
Clearing for housing												
Picnics												
Bushwalking												
Fishing												
Trail-bike riding												
Motor rallies												

What does the matrix tell you? _____

Around the Block

An integrated unit of work about the urban environment

Rationale

Despite the growing interest in and awareness of the natural environment, the majority of people live in an urban, built, environment. For teaching purposes, the urban environment is an immediate and available resource. It offers students a fascinating and accessible area from which to gather data.

As our population grows, urban environments continue to spread at a rapid rate. The operation of all the facilities and services in the urban environment depends on the natural resources available to it. It is true that the lifestyle of those who live in the urban environment is a large contributor to environmental degradation. It is important that students understand the dependence that the urban environment has on the natural environment.

While the urban environment can be seen as a symbol of energy consumption and environmental destruction, we are often blind to this. Our urban environment masks the dependency we have on nature to survive. It 'disconnects' us from the natural environment. Urban environments also tend to be regarded as places that have little or no 'nature' in them; thus we feel less responsibility towards the plants and animals immediately around us.

This unit is not intended to instil in students the notion that urban environments are bad places. Rather it is to develop an awareness that nature does live in the urban environment and that there are ways we can modify our urban environments to better accommodate the natural environment.

By understanding this, it is hoped students will be encouraged to respect, understand and enjoy the environment in which they live and to feel some affection for and responsibility towards it. After all, most of the students we teach will remain urban dwellers for the rest of their lives.

Content

The list below is a summary of the activities that you will find in this unit. It is not suggested that you do them all but that you select some activities from under each major heading to suit your purposes.

Pockets of Nature

Look very closely
And you will find
Pockets of nature
Left behind

Between the cracks
Under a stone
Gently, quietly
She has grown.

About this unit

This unit involves students in a great deal of investigation, monitoring and data collection using their immediate environment. The emphasis is on urban planning. What life exists in our city? How can we look after it? How can we plan to accommodate both nature and the built environment? At the end of the unit, the students work in committee groups to design their own urban environment based on conclusions they have come to after exploring the place in which they live or a town nearby.

There are many environmental issues associated with urban lifestyles. These include pollution, the greenhouse effect, the destruction to the ozone layer, waste and recycling, energy consumption and alternative energy. Intentionally, this unit alludes to, rather than explores, those issues. The unit would, however, provide a good basis for further teaching about such topics.

Understandings

- The urban environment is largely constructed by humans.
- The urban environment has characteristics that distinguish it from rural environments (such as farms) and natural environments (such as rainforests). Urban environments are responsible for much of the pollution that adversely affects the world at large.
- Urban environments are growing and spreading further into natural environments.
- Many things live in the urban environment. Human beings are the dominant species but other living things have their habitats in urban settings.
- We can modify the urban environment and the way we live within it to better care for the plants and animals that share it or that are affected by it.

Key concepts

Change	Future	Domination
Growth and expansion	Development	Lifestyles
Cohabitation	Technology	Population growth
Planning	Dependence	

Skills

Observing	Decision making
Classifying	Creating
Data collection	Comparing
Problem solving	Questioning

"AROUND THE BLOCK" — SAMPLE UNIT PLANNER

Tuning In → Preparing to Find Out → Finding Out → Sorting Out → Going Further → Making Connections → Taking Action

	Session 1	Session 2	Session 3	Session 4	Session 5	Ongoing Activities
Week 1	TUNING IN •Sounds around town	•Reading "31 Ferndale St." •What am I? game	•Set up wildlife observation BLM 1	PREPARING TO FIND OUT •BLM 2 Different environments •Written statements	•What do we do in the city? Drawing & Graphing	•Collect and display posters of urban places
Week 2	•What do we want to find out Group questions	•Writing & phoning for information	•Pre walk-Mapping activity	Tally sheets constructed for each topic area	•constructing surveys for parents and friends	•Survey parents and friends about their City.
Week 3	FINDING OUT •Local walk	•Local walk	SORTING OUT •Oral sharing •Revisit maps	Art •Street Scape	•Street Scape	•Regularly observe city wildlife and note on chart BLM 1
Week 4	Maths •Visual rep. of data collected	•Making a trail	•Making a trail	Drama •Simulation-conflict game BLM 3	•Simulation game •Conflict Matrix BLM 4	•Look in local paper for urban issues
Week 5	Language— Wall story	•Reports & letters after role play	•Responding to reading activities- My Place	GOING FURTHER •Class letter to Town Planner Questions formed	•Visit from Town Planner	
Week 6	Reflection on what has been learnt	MAKING CONNECTIONS •Planning our own town	•Planning our own town.	•Planning our own town.	TAKING ACTION •Discuss and plan a form of local action Reflect on unit	•Monitor various actions decided.

Tuning in

The activities suggested here are designed simply to get students engaged in thinking about the topic. They are designed to sensitise and motivate students . . . to 'get the ball rolling.'

Sounds around town

Ask students to think about all the sounds they might hear if they went out into the yard and listened carefully for a few minutes. They then share ideas with a friend.

Go out into the school yard and say to the students: 'Find a spot by yourself and close your eyes. Listen to all the noises around you. Now make a list of them.'

Return to the classroom and discuss the following: What noises did you hear? Make a descriptive list. What do you think they were? Which ones were human-made? Which ones were natural?'

Repeat the activity (perhaps not with eyes closed!) closer to a busier part of the suburb or in a local park. Compare.

Reading

Read and discuss a picture story book about urban life such as: Jeannie Baker's *Window*, Stewart's *Postcards Home* or Furniss and Abraham's *31 Ferndale Street* (see resource list at the end of the unit.)

Pictures and posters

Bring in posters and other pictures of urban places in different parts of Australia and different parts of the world. (These could be obtained from a local travel agent.) Discuss them using the questions below:

● What things are the same in each?
● What things are different?
● What are the features of urban places?
● What makes up an urban environment?

What am I? (Grouping game)

Play '20 questions'. Each student has a sticker placed on his/her back that has on it an occupation, a plant or animal or a place in the city. Some examples can be found in the table below:

People (occupations)	Animals/plants	Places
police officer	dog	town hall
town planner	cat	supermarket
rubbish collector	sparrow	block of flats
shopkeeper	earwig	house
teacher	spider	shop
pharmacist	seagull	cinema
computer operator	ant	factory
postal officer	possum	post office
	tree	school
	grass	

Students then move around the room asking each other questions to establish their identity. The answers can only be 'yes' or 'no'.

When a student has successfully guessed their identity, they attach their label to their chest. When all the identities of the students have been guessed, play a grouping game. Find some other things that belong with you. Why do they belong together? What other things can you add to your group? Can you form different groups of things that belong together?

Around the Block

Urban animals observation

Begin to gather some data about the animals in and around the school grounds and animals in the students' own living area. A model record sheet is provided in BLM 1. Students could fill out one of these at home and a large replica could be displayed in the classroom to record sightings. Some common urban animals are listed on BLM 6.

Animal	Appearance	Place	Date	Activity	Comments
Bird – Seagull	White and grey with red legs	Outside the milk bar	3-5-90	Fighting for scraps of food with other seagulls	There were 6 in the group – some of the seagulls had brown wings
Caterpillar	Green with red spikes	On the gum tree in the yard.	4-5-90	Eating a leaf	I saw a cocoon too.

Display a map of the local area. A label or sticker could be placed on the map to show the location of various sightings.

At this stage the students can be told that they will be doing a unit of work on the urban environment and that at the end of the unit they will be planning their own town. It will be useful for students to have this task in mind as they engage in the various activities to follow.

Serial reading

Begin to read the book *My Place* by Nadia Wheatley as a class serial. Later in the unit, the students will be engaged in follow-up activities about the book.

Preparing to find out

These activities are designed with three main aims:

1. To give you some insight into what the students already know about the topic and where their initial interests lie;

2. To help students focus clearly on what they already know and what they will try to find out (some activities require the students to make decisions about the ways they will go about gathering information);

3. To prepare the students for the experience to follow (e.g. an excursion) and to focus their investigations.

What do we know about the urban environment?

Students' existing knowledge can be gathered and articulated in a variety of ways.

> People live in an urban environment for employment.
> Ardeer is close to the city
> We can use public transport.
> Ardeer is more peaceful than the city.
> We live near shops, recreation areas and transport.
> When a suburb gets very crowded people move to new areas, making new communities.
> The new community grows larger and larger.
> The paddocks in Fitzgerald Rd may become a new residential area.

> **Rural Environment**
> An urban environment has more residential areas than a rural environment.
> A rural environment is a country or farming environment.
> The rural environment has less pollution than the urban environment.
> A rural environment has an impact on an urban environment.

BLM 2 on p. 113 could be used to begin this activity on an individual or paired basis. The class could then reproduce a large chart that represented their collective ideas.

Students examine the chart that they have made and ask these questions:

- What features are similar to all three types of environments?
- What are the main differences?

These ideas can be illustrated on a giant Venn diagram. This would show the *shared* and *unique* characteristics of each environment.

In pairs or small groups, ask students to write two statements based on the chart. Display these statements with the large chart.

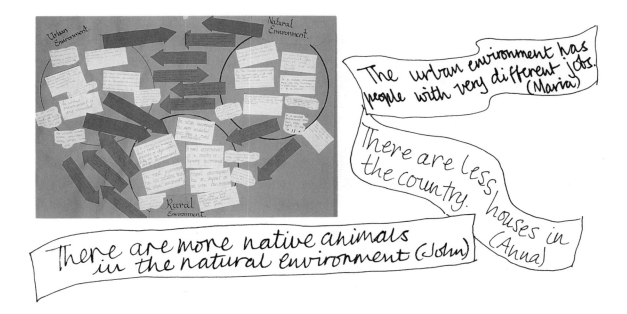

> The urban environment has people with very different jobs. (Maria)

> There are less houses in the country. (Anna)

> There are more native animals in the natural environment (John)

What do we do in the city?

Students divide a page into eight squares. In each square they are asked to illustrate something that is done in the city.

Students then cut out each illustration and share their cards with a group. The group classifies them in some way, perhaps using the categories in the example below. A class chart could then be made using the pictures.

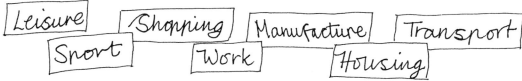

Interviews

Students design some interview questions to ask their parents or friends about living in the city. Below are some suggested questions:

- Why do you live in the city?
- What do you like/dislike about it?
- What changes would you like to see in it?
- Have you ever been to a city in another country? What was it like?

Students write about their findings either individually or in groups using the questions as headings and listing points beneath them.

What do we want to find out?

Divide the students into six groups and ask them to focus their questions about what they want to know using the following sub-topics from which they may choose areas of interest. These groups will be working together at other times in the unit so they should be carefully devised!

- People in the urban environment
- Animals in the urban environment
- Plants in the urban environment
- Buildings in the urban environment
- Transport in the urban environment
- Housing in the urban environment

Share and display questions

How could we find out about these things ? List students' ideas for finding out. No doubt, one of their suggestions will be to write away to people for information (if not, you make it). The places below should provide useful material on the urban environment:

- local town planning office or local council;
- your State Ministry for Planning;
- your urban planning office;
- the Environment Protection Authority in your state
- the department of Conservation and the Environment in your state.

(See also the resource list at the end of the unit.)

Students ring or write to those places requesting information. Requests could be based on their focus questions. To assist them with this task, model a letter to them that could be sent by the whole grade. Alternatively, they could practise their phone call with a partner.

Dear Alan, We are writing this letter to you to ask a few questions about the urban environment. What is your job exactly? How does your job help the urban environment? What suburbs have you been investigating and what problems are you solving at the moment? What have you improved and what has been the effect on the suburb? Have you ever come across a ridiculous complaint and what was it? What do the residents think about your improvements? Thank you for your co-operation.

yours sincerely,
6.M.

Finding out

This experience is designed to give students the opportunity to gather new information about the topic.

A walk around the block

The obvious shared experience for this topic is a walk through the local area. If you are teaching in a country school, you may take a visit to the city for a more intensive study of urban life.

The walk should take in some of the central business district where the traffic is heavier, there are more shops and people. Some of the walk should be through residential areas.

Before the Walk . . .

Mapping

Look at the maps in the book *My Place*. Other maps in children's books can be found in books like Colin Thiele's *Klontarf* (Rigby, 1988) or Nadia Wheatley's *Five Times Dizzy* (Oxford University Press, 1982).

Give the students a defined area of the local environment with which they are familiar. Do this by drawing the street boundaries on the board, e.g. the area bordered by four main streets of the area in which the school and perhaps a local shopping centre is situated.

Ask them to try to draw a map of the area with as much in it as they can recall, within the given boundaries. Is their house in that area? Which direction is their house in? This activity is best done in pairs. Two students can support and assist each other and both participate in the drawing of the map.

Students display maps on a table, walk around and look at each other's maps. Ask them what they missed out and what they need to add to or change on their map. Students have a chance to revise their maps having viewed some of the others' maps. Keep these maps: they will be revisited after the walk.

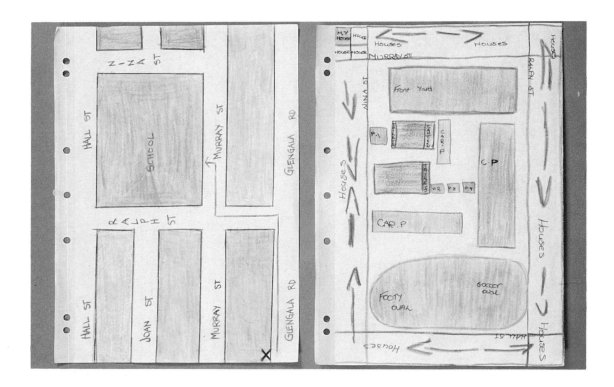

What will we look for?
Your focus area for the walk will depend very much on where your school is situated. However, the students need to spend some time deciding, with your guidance, just what they are going to observe on the walk and how they will keep records. One way to organise it follows.

Students re-form groups according to the topics that they asked questions about. They decide what they want to focus on and how they will gather information. Discuss some strategies with the whole grade first, e.g. surveys, checklists, sketches, photos, notes.

Some ideas for data collection
Animals — Students could focus on, say, birds, and design a tally sheet to record the types and numbers that they see. (Excellent tally sheets are available from the Gould League.)
Plant life — Students take a map with them and plot the areas where plant life is most and least abundant, or they may survey the types of plant life that they see on the walk.

People — This group could note the different activities that people are engaged in around the area. What jobs are they doing? How many are partaking in leisure activities? Again, it may be best for this group to set up a tally sheet before they go out for the walk.

Buildings — Students record the different types, sizes, uses or locations of buildings in the area. They may sketch the buildings on a prepared map.

Housing — Students note the features of the houses in the area (e.g. materials they are made from, styles of houses).

Transport — Students set up a tally sheet to record the different types of vehicles they see.

Alternatively, the walk could be less structured, with each student simply identifying one thing that they will find out or observe on their walk, e.g. things that are natural and things that are human-made; evidence of pollution.

Whatever focus is decided on for the walk, allow the students to make some predictions about the data that they will collect. Make a list of their predictions to return to after the walk.

Take photos of the area that you walk around.

Sorting out

At this stage a variety of activities is suggested across a range of curriculum areas. Students will process information they have gathered and present it in a number of different ways. They may also begin to draw some conclusions about what it is they have learnt.

Initial response to walk

When they return from the walk, students should be given the opportunity to share their findings. They may reform their special interest groups and compare data. They return to their predictions and ask, 'How close were we?' and they return to their questions asked at the start of the unit and ask, 'What do we know now?'

Art

Having made some initial responses to the experience, the students will be ready to express some of their ideas in art. A number of approaches could be used (see below).

Back to our maps

Revisit the map students drew at the beginning of the unit. They re-work the map now that they have actually walked around the area.

A street in the classroom

Students could use a range of materials to reproduce one street or a whole block that was walked around. This reproduction could be in the form of a model, mural, streetscape or collage.

Different groups could work on different streets or areas using the same method of representation. Photos pasted to boxes make a very effective model.

Representing data

Students' art work may focus on the information that they have gathered during the walk. The instruction could be, 'Use the data that you gathered and see if you can make a graph to explain the information.'

Themes

Students might brainstorm particular themes or ideas that they feel emerged from the walk, e.g. the pollution or the different activities of the people.

Students may work alone or in groups. Provide them with a range of materials with which to work (see list on page 192).

Maths

Visual representation of data

Much of the data that students have gathered during the walk will lend itself to graphing and other forms of mathematical visual representation, e.g. the number of houses compared to number of shops compared to number of offices.

Alternatively, students could be asked to gather this sort of quantitative data in their own time in preparation for the activity. This data collection could take the form of a traffic survey (types of road vehicles, number of people in cars, number of cars at different times in the day); or a survey of the birds in the school ground (native, non-native, most to least common); or houses with trees or without trees and so on. The information could be gained through direct observation or through surveying people in the school and other places.

Students spend a week gathering data about one aspect of the urban environments suggested above. All students bring their data to school on a designated day. During this session, students are asked to come up with the best way of showing their data to others. A range of graphing styles should be suggested, e.g. bar graphs, 3-D graphs with blocks, line graphs, pie graphs.

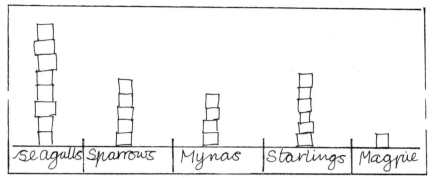

Once graphs have been prepared, share them with the grade. Try to get the students to see patterns in the graphs and speculate about the reasons for those patterns. These general questions could be asked:

- What does the graph tell us?
- What do you think the graph would have looked like twenty years ago?
- What might it look like in twenty years' time?

Specific questions, such as those below, follow:

- Why do you think that the Indian Myna is the most common bird in our urban environment?
- Why do you think that there are so many cars with only one person in them?
- What problems do you think the Indian Myna causes in the urban environment?
- What problems are caused by so many cars with only one driver?

The final question could be, 'What could we do about these things?'

Population

Contact the local council and ask for figures on the town's population etc. Useful information is documented through census statistics. Students could work with these as a basis for graphing or visual representation ideas.

Percentages

Make mathematical summaries of the information gathered through the surveys of people in the local area, e.g. 80% of the people we surveyed enjoyed living in the city. Publish the results in the school newsletter.

Urban trail

Students design a trail for other people through an area of the urban environment. It could be the same route that was taken for the class excursion. The trail must provide *direction* and approximate *distances*. They should assume that the person going on the walk is not familiar with the area. This is an excellent activity for developing students' skills at giving and following directions. They should test the trail out on a friend after school.

Drama

Human sculptures

In groups, students use their bodies to 'sculpt' something that they saw on the walk — it may be an animal, a building or a machine. The other students have to guess the identity of the sculpture. Start with very simple ones, like a letter-box or traffic light. Students could then work in groups to create more complex sculptures.

Interviews

Students work in threes to prepare a TV-style interview between a current affairs host, a city dweller and a country dweller. Groups can perform their interviews to each other.

Simulation exercise

The following activity will need at least two sessions to complete. You should do this activity in a multi-purpose room or hall.

Step 1: Setting the scene. The teacher uses a large roll of poster paper and lays strips out on the floor of the room. The layout could roughly resemble the streets through which the walk has taken place or it could be an imaginary city. Some organising features should be in place before the students enter the room, e.g. labels for parks, shops, streets, the school.

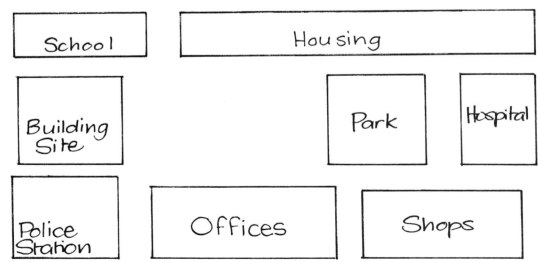

Step 2: Allocation of roles. Students enter the room and are given a role card (sample cards are provided in BLM 3) and a label stating their role to attach to their chest (use sticky labels).

Step 3: Creating the urban environment. Allow students to meet in small groups to discuss their roles. They should give themselves a name and decide what they could be doing once the city swings into action. The students then find a section of the city to which they think they belong and use paints, textas etc. to create their part of the city on the poster paper. As they do this they should be thinking about the role that they play in the city, the job they do, their name etc.

Step 4: Bringing the urban environment to life. When the city is completed, the teacher gives the signal that life in the city should swing into action. Allow the students 5–10 minutes to role-play their daily existence in this city, interacting with each other etc.

Step 5: Causing conflict. Once they are engaged in the activity, the teacher quietly slips into role. You are a developer of a toxic waste plant that will be erected on the outskirts of the town. The plant is needed to store waste from nearby factories. These factories provide employment, goods and revenue for the town. The plant itself will mean that the factories can keep operating. Start measuring the site, perhaps painting a few structural features etc. Eventually the students will begin to ask you questions — explain to them what you are doing and why. The dialogue will no doubt get heated — you need to begin to justify the existence of the plant. Good luck!

Step 6: Talking it through. Suggest that the students hold a public meeting to discuss the issue according to the way that they think their character might feel. You could step out of the role and act as the chair or ask the 'police officer' or 'teacher' to do this.

Step 7: Debriefing. After the session it will be important to debrief the students and explore the way they felt. Use these questions:

- How did you feel being in your role?
- Why do you think you felt that way?
- What made you most angry?
- What other feelings did you have?
- Is there anything you wish you had done or said?

Step 8: Follow-up discussion. Below are some suggested questions:

- What sort of waste products does our urban environment generate?
- Where does it go?
- Is there any 'right place' for waste?
- How can we reduce waste?

Use the conflict matrix (BLM 4) to explore the various conflicts that exist between the environment and urban lifestyles.

Language . . .

Wall story

Write a wall story following the walk or role-play. This story could then be used as the basis for a big book or as the basis for a cloze activity.

Listing

Students list all the things they found in their urban environment. Now tell them to put these words into groups of words that belong together and ask, 'Can we give those groups a label?'

Letter writing

Students write a letter they imagine would be sent to someone about the incident experienced in the role-play. The style of letter will depend on the audience, e.g. some students could write to a friend, some to a newspaper, some students to the Prime Minister and some students could write to the factory manager.

Activities based on My Place
Below are some suggestions for students:

- Imagine your town fifty years ago. Draw a map of what it might have looked like.
- Talk to some elderly people about their memories of the town.
- Find out about your house. When was it built? How old is it?
- Imagine your town in fifty years' time. Draw your ideas about what it might look like in the future.
- Find out who founded your town. What history does it have? Go to the local library and find out.
- Look at the street names around the school. Why do you think those names were chosen?

Going further
These activities are designed to challenge and extend students' understandings. Some may be carried out by the whole group while others are suited to individual or small group research.

Visits to other urban places
Visit another urban place that provides some sort of contrast to yours. If the school is situated in a leafy, residential area, take students to a more industrial area. If your school is in the inner city, take students to an outer suburb.

Make comparative charts, pictures etc. showing the differences and similarities between the two places. Why are they different? What determines the way a town develops?

Country exchange
Students write to a class of students in a country school. They ask them questions about their lives and tell them about their's. (A visit to a country town would obviously be valuable but may not be practical.)

Meet the town planner
Invite a local town planner in to find out more about the place where you live or the place that you walked around. Students interview the town planner and present a report on what they have learnt in the school newsletter.

Step back in time
Visit an elderly person's home or the local senior citizens' club. Students talk to these people about their memories of the town and the changes that have taken place. Role-play and document their interviews when they return.

Open spaces
Using a map of the local area, students measure the area of open space and parkland to the built-up areas. Compare this with other suburbs. Why are there differences?

Friendly designs

Students design an environmentally friendly house for the city. What special features would it have?

Backyard wildlife

Students take a good look at their own garden or backyard. What are the living and non-living things in it? What habitats does their backyard have for urban wildlife? Students design the ideal urban garden.

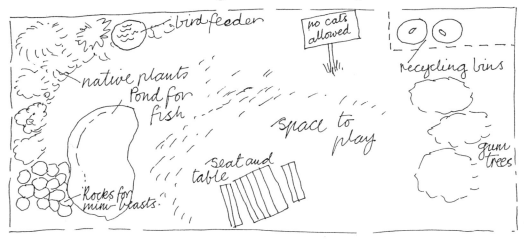

Making connections

At this stage, students will be drawing conclusions about what they have learned. This is an important time for you to evaluate the success of the unit and the needs and achievements of individuals. This is where students 'put it all together'.

What do we know now?

Students can list statements under headings similar to those used in 'What do we want to find out' above. They share statements with each other and challenge/question ideas.

Designing our town

An interesting way to help students 'put it all together' at the end of this unit is to involve them in the process of designing a new urban environment. It would be most useful to begin this process by inviting a local urban environment planner in to talk to the students about his/her job.

Step 1: Setting the scene. Students are allocated to or choose to form particular committees that will oversee the development of a brand new urban environment. Your directive might be, 'Our town has been entirely swept away by a huge tidal wave. We need to re-plan it and we have the opportunity to learn from the mistakes of the past.'

Step 2: Focus questions. What are the current problems that we think our urban environment has? What are the things in the urban environment that we as a grade consider important? What policies will guide our planning?

Step 3: Organising ourselves. Committees form and must adhere to the agreed policies formulated above. The committees (e.g. groups of three) could be responsible for the following:

- housing/residential area;
- shops;
- open space;
- leisure and entertainment;
- waste disposal;
- community services;
- wildlife conservation;
- roads and transport;
- business and the generation of income for the urban environment.

Each group must come up with the following:

- positive and negative points about this aspect of the town (chosen from the list above) as it 'used to be';
- a list of things they consider important for this aspect of the 'new town';
- a plan of how they see their service operating;
- things they will need in order to get started.

The planning sheet presented as BLM 5 will be helpful here.

The jigsaw technique could then be used. A representative from each committee meets to form three large groups. Each representative shares their plans and these questions are discussed:

- What conflicts arise?
- How can we help each other?

Students then return to committees to discuss modifications.

Step 4: Sharing. Each committee displays their plans for 'public comment'. Groups could also represent their area of responsibility visually. Entitle the class display 'Our Place' and invite the school community in to see it.

Taking action

This is a very important element of both the inquiry process and of environmental education. It is essential that students be given opportunities to act upon what they have learnt.

What could we do to improve our urban environment?

Brainstorm ideas and decide on some to put into action. These may include:

- tree planting in the school yard or local community;
- setting up a recycling program;
- starting a clean-up campaign in the school or community;
- keeping an area of native vegetation weeded;
- planting a native area to attract native birds;
- working in the garden at home;
- making a bird feeder for the garden;
- establishing a compost bin;
- continuing the nature diary and asking others in the school to add to it;
- setting up a school-wide competition to design the city of the future (use what you know about the urban environment to judge the winners).

Resources

Children's literature

Anderson, Jan *Towns of Australia* Macmillan 1989
Baker, J. *Home in the Sky* Julia MacRae 1984
Baker, J. *Window* Julia Macrae 1991
Furniss, E. and Abraham, H. *31 Ferndale Street* Macmillan 1989
Stewart, M. *Postcards Home* Macmillan 1990
Tanner, J. *Niki's Walk* Macmillan 1988
Wheatley, N. *My Place* Collins Dove 1988
Young, Noela *Keep Out* Nelson 1984

Teaching resources

Gould League *Urban Survival*
_____ *Urban Discovery Book*
_____ *Environmental Measuring Techniques*
_____ *Monsters and Minibeasts*
Greenall, A. *Taking it to the Streets* (audio-visual kit) Educational Media Australia, Melbourne 1982
National Parks and Wildlife Services of New South Wales. *The Inner City: A Collection of Papers from the Environmental Education Conference* May 1981
Recht, E. *My Place: Teacher's Book* Collins Dove 1990
Rohan, Jones *The Urban Environment as a Wildlife Habitat: Forest and Timber* Forestry Commission of NSW 1980
Scoffham, S. *Using the School's Surroundings* Ward Lock Educational, London, 1980
The Yarra Book: An Urban Wildlife Guide Melbourne Board of Works
Walker, J. and Mitchell, J. *Walmit Divided: A Simulation Game* Curriculum Development Centre, Canberra 1980

Useful contacts

Built Environment Network
Royal Australian Institute of Architects
PO Box 3373
Manuka
NSW 2603

Energy Information Centre (NSW)
33 Playfair Street
The Rocks
NSW 200

Energy Information Centre
139 Flinders Street
Melbourne
Vic. 3000

Watching wildlife
Data collection sheet

Name_____

Animal	Appearance	Place	Time	Activity	Comments
bird – seagull	white and grey with red legs	Outside the milk bar	4·30	Fighting for scraps of food with other seagulls	There were 6 in the group. Some of the seagulls had brown wings

Different environments

Think about the three types of environments listed below. Fill in the chart after you have talked through your ideas with a friend. How are they similar? In what ways are they different?

	Animals	Plants	People	Buildings
Urban (e.g. a city)	There are a lot of dogs and cats and other domestic pets. Birds like seagulls and sparrows are common.			
Rural (e.g. a farm)				
Natural (e.g. a forest)				

Role cards

The cards below can be used in the simulation exercise. Other cards may be designed to suit roles familiar to children in your particular town.

✂ — ✂

teacher
You are the teacher at a local primary school. You live close to the school and know a lot of people in the community. Today you are busy preparing activities for your children.

✂ — ✂

teacher
You are a teacher at the local high school. You teach PE and are a keen sports player. You like to keep fit and healthy.

✂ — ✂

principal
You are the principal of the local primary school. You enjoy living in this town. You have a young family and some of your children go to the school.

✂ — ✂

police officer
You are a senior police officer in the town. You are proud of the town and you think that most people are responsible citizens. You are on traffic duty today.

✂ — ✂

nurse
You work at the local health centre where many people in the community come to see you with their problems. You sometimes work in the casualty section of the local hospital.

✂ — ✂

shopkeeper
You own a newsagency in the town and have a busy job serving customers, organising paper rounds and running your business. You do not live in this town. You prefer to live elsewhere and drive to work each day.

✂ — ✂

shopkeeper
You own a small fruit and vegetable stall in the town. You grow a lot of your own food and like to think that you can offer people fresh, chemical-free produce.

✂ — ✂

✂ — ✂

conservation officer
You are in town today because a rare species of lizard has been discovered living near the old railway yards. You are hoping to find out more about the lizard and to see what other animals can be found around the town.

✂ — ✂

environmentalist
You are a member of a local group that is concerned about the environment. You are particularly worried about the health of your children and you think that there should be less pollution in the air and water. You live in the area and today you are getting ready for a meeting about the pollution problem.

✂ — ✂

real estate agent
You sell houses, offices and land in the town. You are pleased that lots of people seem to be moving to the town — you think that it is a good place to live and work.

✂ — ✂

gardener
You have been a gardener at the town park for many years. Many people use the park for picnics, walks and other leisure activities. You have noticed that some of the trees are not as healthy as they used to be and you worry about the pollution in the air.

✂ — ✂

factory worker
You work in a local factory and have to earn money to support a large family. You are proud of the products that your factory makes and you know that what you do is important for your town.

✂ — ✂

construction worker
You are a construction worker. You live in the town and you do lots of different jobs. At the moment you are working on a new building in the city centre.

✂ — ✂

child
You are a child who has just moved to the town. Your parents have just rented a house and you really like living here. You have asthma but so far it has not been too bad in this town.

✂ — ✂

Around the Block

✂ — ✂

child
You are a child who has lived here since you were born. Your dad is the principal of the local school. Your favourite game is cricket — you are on the school team.

✂ — ✂

factory manager
You are the manager of a local factory. You are worried about the waste that the factory produces. You are trying to think of ways in which it can be stored. You know that it is dangerous if not handled properly.

✂ — ✂

newspaper editor
You are the local newspaper editor and you are always looking for a good story!

✂ — ✂

mayor
You are the town mayor. It is your job to make sure that any problems in the town are sorted out. You are a friendly person and know almost everyone in the town.

✂ — ✂

unemployed person
You have left school and are looking for a job. You visit the CES every day but you haven't had much luck. You would be happy to do any job. You want to save up to buy a car.

✂ — ✂

parent
You have just had a new baby and you are staying at home to look after it. You think that this is a good town to bring up children — you were born here too.

✂ — ✂

elderly person
You are eighty-five years old and you have lived in this town all your life. You have seen many things change and think that some changes have been good while others have not been so good for the town. You take your dog for a walk to the shops every day.

✂ — ✂

Conflict matrix

This grid is called a conflict matrix. You can use it to help sort out the things that you think are good or bad for cities and the living things (including people!) in them. On the top of the matrix are some of the changes in many cities. Down the side of the matrix are things that the city is used for. You have to decide if these things go together or if they cause conflict. (Read each use of the city and then look at the change to see what effect you think it will have.)

Read the grid like a map. Write your ideas in the spaces provided. Some have been done for you.

		Changes				
		more traffic	more people	more parks	more cats	more pollution
Uses of the city	a place for people to work					
	habitat for some native animals and birds	Traffic might pollute the air – the birds could get sick.				
	place for recreation and leisure (e.g. sport)			More places for picnics, walks, sport		People might get sick (e.g. asthma) when they are playing sport
	place for people to live					
	a tourist attraction					

Committee planning sheet

Name of committee:_____

Members:_____

_____

_____

_____

_____

_____

_____

_____

_____

What ideas do you have for your area?_____

_____

_____

_____

_____

_____

_____

_____

_____

_____

_____

_____

How will your ideas be put into place? _____

_____

_____

_____

_____

What rules will you have for your area? _____

_____

_____

_____

_____

What problems might you have in this area? _____

_____

_____

_____

_____

_____

_____

_____

_____

_____

Around the Block

Common urban animals

Reptiles
marbled gecko
grass skink
blue-tongued lizard
tiger snake

Amphibians
green tree frog (in warmer states)
brown tree frog

Birds
Indian myna
seagull
starling
sparrow
magpie
magpie lark
kookaburra
plover (spur-winged)
white-plumed honey eater
wattle bird
blackbird
rosella

Insects
ant
bee
mosquito
caterpillar
butterfly
dragonfly
earwig
wasp
moth
beetle
termite
cricket
grasshopper

Spiders

daddy-long-legs
golden orb weaver
huntsman
redback
wolf spider

Mammals

cat
dog
possum
bat
Antechinus (a small marsupial mouse)

Using this list

- The illustrations may assist children with identification when completing their wildlife observation sheets (BLM 1).
- Present a list of the animals to the children and ask them to classify them in some way, e.g. native/introduced; according to animal grouping; according to habitat or where found.

Around the Block

An Oasis of Life

An integrated unit of work about wetlands

Rationale

Wetlands teem with life. They provide shelter for many species of water birds, reptiles, fish, amphibians, mammals and countless invertebrates. Wetlands are enormously valuable habitats and as much a part of the Australian environment as the arid terrain that we are perhaps more famous for. In a country where water supply is relatively scarce, wetlands are indeed worth understanding and conserving.

A wetland can be a true oasis for animals and humans alike. For many students, a wetland area can provide hours of adventure and discovery as they find tadpoles or yabbies, sit and listen to the call of frogs or watch insects dart over the surface of the water. Wetlands are peaceful and often accessible places from which students can learn much about their environment.

Over the past 200 years, much of Australia's precious wetland areas have been lost through activities such as clearing of vegetation, inappropriate farming practices, urban development, dam construction, waste disposal and drainage. Few of Australia's wetland areas remain in their original state. Many wetlands have been modified since European settlement and no longer support the life that they once did.

We need to understand and care for the wetlands that remain.

Contents

The list below is a summary of the activities that you will find in this unit.
It is not suggested that you do them all but that you select some activities
from under each major heading to suit your purposes.

Pond
Still, dark
Glistening, soothing, humming
Brimming with life beneath
Oasis

About this unit

Through this unit of work on wetlands, students will develop understandings about habitat, food chains and the effect of human activity on natural areas. Many students will have had the experience of visiting some sort of wetland area. If not, this unit should provide them with that experience. There are many places that teachers can take students to show them a wetland first-hand. In fact, this unit is designed around the *direct experience of visiting a wetland area* and uses that experience to develop understandings about the topic. It is also hoped that, through the unit, an emphasis will be placed on the simple enjoyment that one can gain from being out in the natural environment.

For the purposes of this unit, wetlands will not include ocean or beach areas.

Understandings

- Wetlands are important ecosystems within the total environment.
- There are many plants and animals that rely on wetlands to survive.
- The life in a wetland is linked together in a complex web of relationships.
- There are different types of wetlands.
- Human activity since European settlement has caused the degradation of many of Australia's wetlands.
- There are things that we can do to better care for our wetlands.

Key concepts

Interrelationships   Adaptation
Interdependence   Survival
Habitat   Cause and effect
Preservation   Ecosystem
Food webs

Skills

Observation
Data collection
Recording information
Problem solving
Decision making
Co-operating
Analysing data
Creative thinking

"AN OASIS OF LIFE" — SAMPLE UNIT PLANNER

Tuning in → Preparing to find out → Finding out → Sorting out → Going Further → Making Connections → Taking Action

	Session 1	Session 2	Session 3	Session 4	Session 5	Ongoing Activities
Week 1	TUNING IN · Picture Puzzle · Visualisation	· Story: Black Duck and Water Rat · Listing wet places What is a wetland?	PREPARING TO FIND OUT · What do we know about wetlands? 4 groups brainstorm focus questions	· Planning our excursion. Allocating tasks.	· Organising aspects to investigate. Investigation Sheet – BLM 1	· Begin class serial "The Magic Finger" - Roald Dahl
Week 2	· Preparing for excursion Gathering and making materials etc.	FINDING OUT · Visit to wetland and related activities BLM 2	· Visit to wetland and related activities	· Visit to wetland and related activities	SORTING OUT · Initial response sharing in topic then mixed topic groups.	· Children keep reflective journals about the various activities in the unit.
Week 3	Art · Class mural of wetland	· Using wet paper and chalk — representation of wetland	Language · Model report writing using a factual text Draft reports	· Write group reports of investigation.	· Individual retrieval charts. Whole class chart.	· Build list of key words about wetlands. Use in word study.
Week 4	Literature · "Longnecks Billabong" Shared book activities	· "Longneck's Billabong" Review understandings	Drama · duck shooting "In Their Shoes"	· Conflict Matrix BLM 3	GOING FURTHER · Planning for our own classroom wetland	· Set up observation tasks for wetlands area
Week 5	· Building the wetland	· Building the wetland Complete class 'how to' chart	· Maths activities to find out about class wetland	· Visual representation of maths activities	MAKING CONNECTIONS · Concept mapping "What we know now"	· Invite others in to see wetland — give talks.
Week 6	TAKING ACTION · Shared Book "Lester & Clyde" How do humans harm wetlands	· Discuss and brainstorm personal action.	· Plan and carry out chosen action.	· Plan and carry out chosen action.	· Reflect on the Unit	· Literature activities for "Lester & Clyde"

Comments:

Tuning in

The activities suggested here are designed simply to get students engaged in thinking about the topic. They are designed to sensitise and motivate students . . . to 'get the ball rolling'.

Picture puzzle

Use a poster that depicts a wetlands scene. There are many available through local water authorities and government departments of environment and conservation. Attach the poster to the blackboard or some other solid surface. Cover the poster with a sheet of card that has been cut into separate jigsaw-type pieces each piece is attached with Blu-Tack. Slowly remove each piece to reveal portions of the poster, asking the students what they think the poster is about. The smaller the pieces, the more challenging the task.

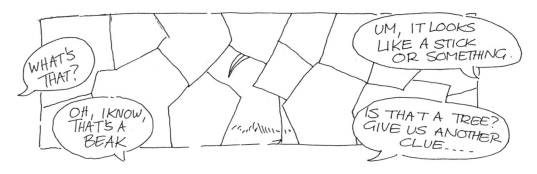

Class serial

Begin the unit by reading *The Magic finger* by Roald Dahl or *Storm Boy* by Colin Thiele. These books can be used as the basis for drama activities about hunting later in the unit.

Picture story book

Read *Black Duck* and *Water Rat* by Percy Trezise and Mary Haginikitas. This Aboriginal myth is set in a wetland environment and will provide an interesting stimulus for discussion. Another good starter is *The Frog and the Pelican* by D. O'Brien.

Visualisation

Ask students to close their eyes and imagine that they are in a wetland environment. Provide some clues for them, e.g. It is a 'soggy' place, you

have your gum boots on so that you don't get wet. There are lots of water reeds around the edge of your wetland. It is quiet but you can hear the sounds of frogs calling to each other.' Students open their eyes and, in pairs, share the things that they 'saw' on their visit to a wetland. They may ask each other questions like, 'What did you see? What sounds did you hear? What did it smell like? Were you hot or cold?'

Preparing to find out
These activities are designed with three main aims:
1. To give you some insight into what the students already know about the topic and where their initial interests lie;
2. To help students focus clearly on what they already know and what they will try to find out. Some activities require the students to make decisions about the ways they will go about gathering information;
3. To prepare the students for the experience to follow (e.g. an excursion) and to focus their investigations.

Now that the students have done some initial thinking about the topic, it is time to find out what they already understand about wetlands.
This can be done in a variety of ways.

Wet places
Ask students: 'What "wet places" do we know around our area? Make a list of these and the things that are found there'.

Place	What's found there
Korroroit Creek	rubbish, flies, some tadpoles, birds (mostly seagulls), people
Pool	people, some birds
Sanctuary	lots of different birds, fish, frogs and tadpoles, water beetles, people

After constructing the chart together, discuss the following:
● What do all these wet places have in common?
● In what ways are they different?

Listing

Make a list of different types of wetlands. At this stage, use the names that students offer to describe them.

A wetland can be defined as . . . 'areas of marsh, fen, peatland or water whether natural or artificial, permanent, seasonal or cyclical with water that is static or flowing, fresh, brackish or salt, including mudflats and mangrove areas exposed at low tide (Department of Conservation Forest and Lands Vic. *Highlights of Victoria's Wetlands Conservation Program*, p. 2).

As the name suggests, a wetland is a place where an area of land is covered by water. They are generally thought of as shallow places rather than deep bodies of water like rivers or lakes.

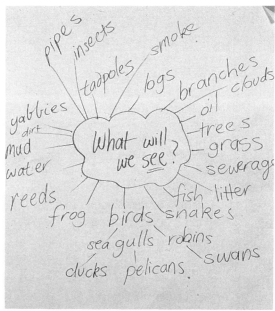

Decide on a definition of a wetland. This can be done by asking each student to complete the phrase, 'A wetland is . . . ' Then compile ideas onto a class chart. What do we know? What words do you think of when you think about wetlands?

These words can be listed and grouped under headings.

What do we know?

Divide students into four groups. Each focus question below will be looked at by a group. They may respond through words or pictures or both.

- What kinds of animals and plants live in wetlands?
- What do humans use wetlands for?
- What are the things that can harm wetlands?
- What are the features of wetlands?

Individual groups brainstorm.

Two groups with the same questions amalgamate and come up with a common list.

Display four lists and share. Ask, 'Are there things we are sure about? (Underline these in one colour.) Are there things we are not sure about? (Underline these in another colour.)'

At this stage, you should decide on an excursion site to be identified for a shared experience. For information on wetland areas in your state, see useful contacts section on page 196.

Once you have decided on a place to visit, it is important that you gather some information about it yourself so that you know what possibilities there are for students' investigations.

It should be a place where the students will be able to observe some wildlife and, ideally, be able to take some small samples of water. If this is not possible, many zoos or wildlife parks have simulated wetland environments that the students could visit.

If you are unable to conduct an excursion, contact the media section of your state education department. There are a number of excellent videos and slide sets available. These include:

- *Billabong and Waterhole* Educational Media Australia, 1978;
- *Receding Wetlands* (Northern Territory) Australian Broadcasting Corporation documentary;
- *Marsh and Mangrove* (Victoria) Australian Broadcasting Corporation (Wild Australia Series);
- *The Wetlands Problem* Educational Media Australia.

Planning the excursion

As a way of giving a 'real life' context for your integrated unit, a very
valuable exercise is to involve the students in the planning of the class
excursion.The following steps are a guide to the way you might go about
doing this. It is suggested that different students or groups of students are
allocated various responsibilities in the preparation.

Once a place has been decided on, ask the students: What are all the
things that we will need to do to organise our visit to a wetland?

```
*Find out how much it will cost.
*Find out how to get there.
*Estimate travel time, decide on best route.
*Book the bus.
*Decide on a suitable date and time.
*Get permission from the school council.
*Write a letter to parents for permission & to explain what
                                              we are doing.
*Ask some parents to come along.
*Organise lunch.
*Find out about the place and what we need to bring & wear.
*Decide on some things to do and find out about when we
                                              get there.
```

Students can now be allocated appropriate roles and tasks from the list.
Many of these tasks will provide useful practice in maths and language
skills.

Organising the investigations

It is important that students see a real purpose for their visit to the wetland
and that they are engaged in some sort of data gathering when they are
there. Return to the categories brainstormed earlier in the unit. Ask
students to list some questions about that area. Alternatively, each student
could list one question and then groups could form on the basis of common
interests.

```
Animals and Plants
What types of birds are there at the creek?
What types of insects are there?
Are the animals protected?
Where do most of the animals live?
Do all the animals live in the water?
```

Humans
How do humans use the creek?
Do people fish there?
Are there rules for people at the creek?
Why do people go there?

Threats to wetlands
Is there pollution in the creek?
Does it smell?
Is there rubbish there?
Are there any bits that look unhealthy?

Features
What shape is the wetland?
What colour is the water?
What sorts of plants are there?
Is there sand on the banks?
How deep is the water?

How will we find out?

This is an important aspect of the unit. As students are engaged in problem solving, hypothesising and co-operating, they come up with ways they will investigate their questions.

From the questions gathered, students (in the same topic groups) select some to focus on. They can then use BLM 1 (p. 146) to formally develop their ideas for investigation.

As a grade, discuss what you expect the wetland to be like.

Students could produce some art work to illustrate their ideas about the wetland before the visit or video.

Some useful materials for your visit to the wetland are:

- dip nets can be made by stretching stockings over a wire coat hanger;
- magnifying glasses;
- plastic containers with lids;
- buckets;
- ground sheet to sit on;
- clear plastic pocket to store activity cards;
- clip-boards;
- non-permanent pens that can write on plastic;
- pencils;
- tape recorder for wetland noises;
- camera;
- identification charts for invertebrates, birds and insects (all available from the Gould League).

Finding out

These experiences are designed to give students the opportunity to gather new information about the topic.

Visiting a wetland

BLM 2 on page 147 (Getting to know Wetlands) has some suggested activities that may assist students in their investigations. These activities would be further enhanced if used with the charts and survey sheets available from the Gould League in your state. This would assist students in identifying the plants and animals that they discover.

Some wetland areas may be set aside in your state for educational purposes. If this is the case there may be an educational officer on site who could assist you with developing some class activities as well as allowing time for students to gather their data.

Give students some 'wandering and exploring' time too! At some time in the day, ask them all to find one special spot in the area and sit there, quietly and alone for a while.

Make sure that you take some photographs of the various things that you see and do. These will provide a useful record of the area and a resource for activities when you return.

Ensure that you are all dressed suitably for the excursion. Gum boots are a must! It is also a good idea to take a sturdy piece of plastic for each student to sit on. These can be used again and again for outdoor activities.

Sorting out

At this stage a variety of activities is suggested across a range of curriculum areas. Students will process information they have gathered and present it in a number of different ways. They may also begin to draw some conclusions about what it is they have learnt.

Summarising data

On returning from the excursion, students should first complete their various investigation sheets.

Groups take it in turns to report on the things that they found out. One way of doing this is to organise the groups so that there is a representative from each investigation (humans, animals and plants, threats, features). Each person reports on what they discovered.

Information should be added to the original four lists that were devised at the initial stages of the unit.

Art

Students represent their experience using art. This may be a general response or specific to the students' investigations. They may show something they saw at the wetland or show their findings using a variety of art materials.

You may suggest some 'watery' art for the above activities, such as using water colours, drawing with chalk on wet paper, using a weak solution of paint and water to wash over picture done in pastel.

Mural

Re-create one of the areas that you studied in detail by preparing a mural of the wetland. Label the mural when complete.

Photo art

Use the photos to display various aspects of the wetland area. An effective technique is to mix students' own art work with the photos, e.g. you may have a photo of a bird: paste it to a page and draw its habitat around it.

Models

Make models of the wetland area that you visited. Use natural materials such as bark, grass, twigs and rocks (only those found on the ground) to bring the model to life. Return the materials when you have finished displaying the model.

Language

Writing up investigations
Written reports based on investigations.

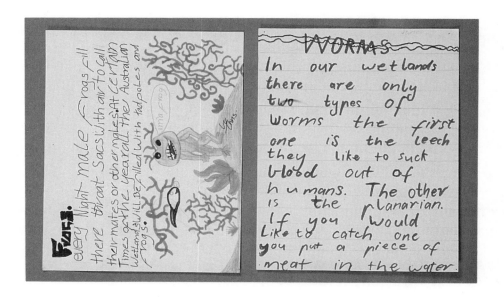

A class report
Write a class report for the school newsletter about your visit to the wetland. Do this as a class using a wall story technique.

On Thursday, 3rd of September, grade 3M visited the wetlands at 'Pipe-makers park.' We found out many things about wetlands. Birds need wetlands for food and shelter. We saw swamp hens in the reeds. The wetlands are only 'wet' during certain times of the year. People need to be quiet near the wetlands.

This report can also be used as the basis for other language activities such as cloze, sentence reconstruction, sequencing of sentences and word substitution.

Photographic records

Use the photographs to compile a class book about the particular wetland that you visited. To assist students in writing the text to accompany photos, examine a range of published texts that deal with factual information about the wetland environment (see resource list under 'general information about wetlands').

Analyse the style of language that authors use in factual books.
Encourage students to use this sort of language in their own writing.

Wetlands have plants that are designed to float. They often have big flat leaves.

Clue cards

Students devise clues through which others must guess a wetland creature, for example: I have long legs; I have white feathers; I have a beak with a spoon shape at the end; What am I?
These clues are written on the outside of folded cards. On opening the card, the answer will be found written and illustrated inside.

Retrieval chart

Compile a retrieval chart comparing three different types of environments. Select environments that you think students would be familiar with. BLM 3 is provided on page 148. Students can complete this chart individually or in pairs before compiling a class list.

	Animals	Plants	Human uses	Threats
Environment 1: Wetlands	Water birds frogs fish	reeds algae	Swimming fishing	pollution waste sewage
Environment 2: Forests	possums lizards	gum trees tree ferns	wood walking	logging
Environment 3: City	Cats dogs Sparrows	flowers grass	working living	pollution too crowded

Using information from the retrieval chart, students write generalisations about the four aspects. The teacher may need to model some of these generalisations first.

Ask, 'What does the chart tell us?'

Wetlands can be a nightmare for animals.

People go to the wetlands to listen to animal noises.

People fish for sport.

Different environments have different animals in them.

Literature

Longneck's Billabong (see resource list) is an excellent picture story book that promotes students' understanding of wetlands as 'teeming with life' and of the important interrelationships between the plants and animals in a wetland environment. Below is a series of activities that could be undertaken when using this book with students.

Predictions

Divide the group into three (or six) smaller groups. Each will take on an activity that will help prepare them for the information in the book. Groups should nominate a recorder (to take down information), a reporter (to share with class) and an observer (to monitor the co-operative behaviour of the group).

These are the tasks for each group:

● Group 1: Draw/write everything you know about billabongs. List some questions you have about them.
● Group 2: Draw/write everything you know about tortoises. List some of the questions you have about them.
● Group 3: Use cards with animal names to try and construct a food web. With Blu-Tack, place the cards on the white board and put arrows to connect food chains.

After each group has finished their task they should report back to the rest.

At this stage, accept approximations and hypotheses. It is important that it is the learners themselves who challenge their ideas after they have been given further information.

Read the big book *Longneck's Billabong*. Now review predictions: students ask themselves whether they were right and add or delete information.

Story map

Students create a pictorial map of the story of Longneck's life. The map can use words and pictures to show the sequence of Coleridge's story

Discuss and list as a class answers to the question: 'What did Anne Coleridge need to know about billabongs and tortoises to write this book?'

Questions and statements about wetlands should also be reviewed at this stage. Ask, 'What do we know now?'

Drama

Activities related to serial book

It is assumed that the book *The Magic Finger* or *Storm Boy* has been read to the students. Duck shooting is a quite controversial issue to explore with young students. However, it is one that receives much exposure through the media and is an activity that affects wetlands in many ways. It is a useful vehicle through which to conduct activities that help students understand the range of values held in our society and the reasons behind the variety of viewpoints held about environmental issues.

Below are some related drama activities:

- Paired interviews with a character from the book.

- Mini-scenes selected from the book and performed by small groups of students.
- Mini debate: Fishing or Duck Shooting? What's the difference?
- Interviewing a range of people about duck shooting: parents, grandparents etc.

Putting on different shoes

This activity, based on Edward De Bono's idea of 'coloured hats', is designed to get students thinking in a range of ways about one issue. They could do the activity individually or in pairs.

Ask them to divide a page into six squares.

The angry shoes
- In the first square, write down something about duck shooting that makes you feel angry

The happy shoes
- In the second, write something about duck shooting you feel positive about

The factual shoes
- In the third, some facts you know about duck shooting

The puzzled shoes
- In the fourth, write some questions you have about it — things you are puzzled about

The creative shoes
- In the fifth square, write something you think might help solve the conflict

The realistic shoes
- In the sixth square, write what you really think will happen about duck shooting in the future.

In groups of six, each student presents ideas in one 'pair of shoes'. They may do this verbally or using mime. Students could take on a role to match each pair of shoes: happy — duck shooter; angry — conservationist; factual — scientist; puzzled — average citizen; solving — ranger.

Wetlands and conflict

Use the BLM 4 'Living with Wetlands' to think through the way humans use wetlands and the potential destruction of their tenuous ecosystem. Prepare mini-scenes in groups to illustrate one of the conflicting situations.

Going further

These activities are designed to challenge and extend students' understanding about the topic.

Making our own wetland

You will need:

- an aquarium or small children's wading pool;
- rocks;
- soil or gravel;
- water plant (available from pet shops and aquariums). Try to avoid non-native species as they can infect wetland areas if taken to them. Ask for native plants (e.g. fast-growing azolla).
- water! (if using water from a tap, you should let it stand for a time before using it);

- water purifier if necessary;
- suitable water creatures such as tadpoles, yabbies, water beetles.
- (if collected from wetland, return at the end of the activity);
- filter;
- sunlight.

Explain to students that they are going to make their own wetland inside the classroom. Before constructing the wetland, students could design their version of what it could look like and what could be in it. Some suggestions are yabbies; tortoises; tadpoles; small water organisms (beetles etc.). Display students' designs and select popular features.

One way of organising the creation of this sort of display is to have very small groups of students working there on a rotational basis. Each group could be assigned a given task, such as group 1 lays the gravel and rocks, group 2 is responsible for placing the plants, group 3 is in charge of filters and group 4 has responsibility for the animals.

Be quiet near our wetland
Please do not move the rocks.
3 people at a time.

When the wetland environment is finished, some rules for its maintenance should be agreed upon. It should also be understood that the creatures will be with you for only a short time and that they will be returned to their natural habitat upon completion of the unit.

N.B. You should check your state's regulations on keeping animals in the classroom before undertaking this activity.

Related measurement activities

Measure the temperature of the water daily or at different times in a day. Plot the results on a graph. Discuss reasons for variations.

Mark the level of water when the wetland is first made. Note the amount that the level drops each day. Again, this information could be recorded on a graph.

Observe the living things that are in the wetland. Note their preferred positions at different times in the day. Plot these on a sketch of your wetland.

Monitor the growth of the azolla (water weed). Count the individual plants each day and keep a record of the growth in numbers. What factors seem to influence the growth of the azolla?

Other extension ideas . . .

If videos were not viewed as a shared experience, this would be an opportunity to view one. (See p. 129.)

Look at maps of the town or state that students live in. Where are the main wet areas? Why? Look at a map of Australia and do the same. Where are the main river systems in each state?

Visit another wetland in a different place and compare it to the one that you studied.

Watch the film of *Storm Boy* and compare with the book. How are salty wetlands different from fresh ones?

Making connections

At this stage, students will be drawing conclusions about what they have learnt. This is an important time for you to evaluate the success of the unit and the needs and achievements of individuals. This is where students 'put it all together'.

Concept mapping

This technique is an effective way to assess the students' understandings about wetlands and to guide any further planning. One approach to concept mapping is detailed below:

- Give students ten small cards.
- On one card, they write the word 'wetlands'.
- On the remaining cards they write any words or draw pictures about wetlands that they think are the most important ones.
- Provide them with big sheets of paper. Their task is to organise the cards on the paper in a way that makes sense to them.
- They then have to show how those words relate to each other. This is done with a series of lines connecting the cards. Words or phrases are written on the lines to make the connection clearer.
- The cards can be stuck on with Blu-Tack so that they can be re-organised as the map is formed.
- Ask students then to share their map with a friend and ask, 'What does your friend understand by your map?'
- Finally, students use their maps to form generalisations about wetlands. These can be displayed and shared.

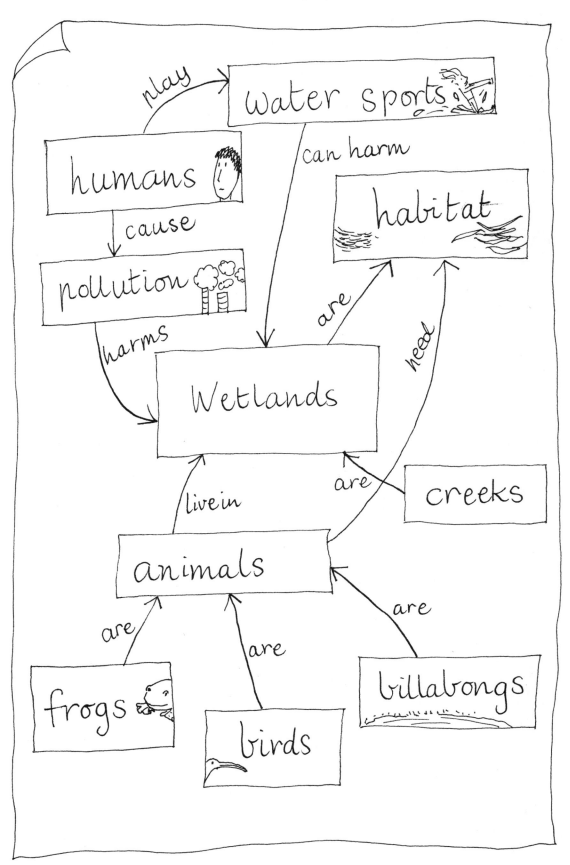

Taking action

This is a very important element of both the inquiry process and of environmental education. It is important that students be given opportunities to act upon what they have learnt.

Lester and Clyde

One way to round the unit off and further stimulate students to act would be to read the big book edition of *Lester and Clyde* (see resource list for details). Pose these questions: What problems did the humans bring to this wetland? Why? What problems did we see at our wetland? What problems do wetlands face?

Whole grade action

Using the information gained through the unit of work, students should now have a degree of understanding both of the importance of wetlands and of the threat to them by human misuse. Discuss together something that they could do based on the knowledge that they have.

Below are some examples of whole grade action:

● Visit a local wetland that may be littered and have a clean-up session.

● Mount a campaign in the school or community to explain the importance of wetlands.
● Invite others to see your classroom wetland and give short talks about it. Set up an information display.
● Write to the local council about the protection or upkeep of a local creek, river, pond etc.
● What would you do about wetlands if you were in government?

Resources

Children's literature

Coleridge, M. *Longneck's Billabong* Macmillan 1987 (big book format available)

Howes, J. *Down Round About and up Again: The Story of a River* Macmillan 1987

O'Brien, D. *The Frog and The Pelican* Fontana 1981

Reece, J. *Lester and Clyde* Ashton Scholastic 1976

Thiele, Colin *Storm Boy* Rigby 1976

Thiele, Colin *The Magic Finger* Puffin 1974

Tresize, P. and Haginikitas, M. *Black Duck and Water Rat* Collins 1988

Teaching resources

Gould League *Wetlands Wildlife: The Nature of Wetlands in Southern Australia* 1989. The Gould League has many excellent resources for teaching about wetlands. Contact your state office for a catalogue.

Kakadu Billabong (CD and cassette) by Les Gilbert; 60 minutes, 1990 (available from Wilderness Society)

Miller, R. *Fresh Water Invertebrates* Gould League

NSW National Parks and Wildlife Services *Wetlands (Teacher's Kit)* 1984 (available from NSW NPWS, 189 Kent Street, Sydney)

Survival: Swamps and Streams Gould League

General information about wetlands

Birds of the Maribyrnong Valley Friends of the Maribyrnong River 1988

Cowling, S. J. 'Wetland Habitats' in *Birds of Victoria: Inland Waters* pp. 7–10, Gould League of Vic.

Fairley, A. *River and Stream* Methuen 1982

Fox, A. and Parish, S. *Of Birds and Billabongs* Rigby 1983

Haigh, C. (ed.) *Wetlands in NSW* NSW National Parks and Wildlife Services

Jones, W. *The Wetlands of the South-East of South Australia* Nature Conservation Society of South Australia

Miller, R. *Fresh Water Invertebrates* Gould League

The Yarra Book: An Urban Wildlife Guide Melbourne and Metropolitan Board of Works

Wetlands investigations planner

Name(s)_____

_____

What do we want to find out? (List questions)_____

_____

_____

_____

_____

How will we find out?_____

_____

_____

_____

_____

What equipment do we need?_____

_____

How will we record the information that we gather?_____

_____

_____

What do we expect to find out?_____

_____

_____

_____

_____

Results_____

_____

_____

_____

Comments_____

_____

_____

_____

_____

Getting to know wetlands

Listening post — natural and artificial sounds

Find a place to sit where your group can be away from the others.

When you are ready and comfortable, spend two minutes listening to the sounds of the wetland. Focus on the natural sounds. Talk about what you heard. You will probably have noticed different things.

Now do it again — this time, focus on the sounds that are made by artificial or people-made things. Tell each other what your favourite sound was and why.

Now, can you see where the sounds were coming from?

Mini-trail

Lay your piece of string out in a line across an area close to the edge of the wetland that you think would be interesting to study. With the help of a magnifying glass, see if you can discover what things live along the string line. Can you see evidence of any minibeast life? What sort of habitats can you see? Watch your area closely. Is anything moving? Does anything in your area change as you watch it?

Now find a different spot to mark out further away from the edge. Do the same thing here. What things are the same? What things are different? Why?

Bird watch

Find a spot near the wetland where you think you might be able to see some birds. Talk to each other about the sorts of birds you think you will see here and why. Where do you think they might live?

Now spend some time just watching. If you see a bird, make a very quick sketch of what it looks like. Is it big? Small? What colour is it? Look at the beak and feet that the bird has. What is the bird doing? Why? Watch it for as long as you can and make some notes about what you see.

Pond search

What sort of small creatures do you think might live in the water?

Use the nets or containers to collect some water from the edge of the pond. Empty it into the container. What have you found?

Now collect some from further in or deeper down. Have you found anything new? Show each other what you have found.

How many different sorts of creatures were there? What do they have in common? Use a magnifying glass to help you study the things more closely.

When you have finished, return the water to the wetland.

Different environments

	Animals	Plants	Human uses	Threats
Environment 1: _____				
Environment 2: _____				
Environment 3: _____				

Living with wetlands

Use this grid to think about the things people do in wetlands. What things threaten wetlands? (Some have been done for you.)

	Disposal of waste	Boating	Swimming	Duck shooting	Bird watching
Habitat for birds					
Source of fresh water					
Place for peaceful recreation					

149

On Behalf of the Other Animals

An integrated unit of work about threatened animals.

Rationale

The issue of threatened, endangered and extinct animals of the world is one that easily captures the hearts and the imaginations of students and adults alike. While extinction is a natural process, the speed at which it has occurred since the evolution of humans (particularly over the last 100 years) is alarming and indeed significant.

Although students will identify quickly with the threat to creatures such as the beautiful giant panda bear, the issue of threatened species must extend far beyond the plight of the 'cute and cuddlies'. The activities of humans upon this planet have led to widespread destruction of all kinds of life on earth — from birds and mammals to plants and insects. The threat to those very life forms at the base of the food chain (the plants and invertebrates) is most disturbing. The loss of one plant species, for example, could put at risk many animals that are dependent on it and, in turn, other life forms dependent on the animals.

Species loss, however, is about much more than the simple disappearance of plants and animals from the planet. The extinction of a fellow living thing from the planet is a stark reminder of the transience of nature and the impact that we humans can have upon it. Many scientists predict that we may be entering an age of the 'lonely planet' where, in our zest to develop and control the environment, we may lose the company of those with whom we share the planet — the other animals.

Contents

The list below is a summary of the activities that you will find in this unit. It is not suggested that you do them all but that you select some activities from under each major heading to suit your purposes.

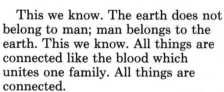

This we know. The earth does not belong to man; man belongs to the earth. This we know. All things are connected like the blood which unites one family. All things are connected.

Whatever befalls the earth befalls the sons of the earth. Man did not weave the web of life; he is merely a strand in it. Whatever he does to the web, he does to himself . . .

Attributed to Chief Seattle

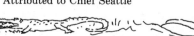

About this unit

This unit is most effective when students already have some existing understandings about habitat and the nature of interdependence between living things. Activities are designed to challenge students' values and attitudes, to encourage them to empathise with and develop some feeling of responsibility for the fellow tenants of earth. Similarly, it aims to develop important skills of research through data collection, reporting and analysis. This is done through direct experience and through reading.

Although this unit focuses on animals, reference is made to threatened plants, which is as important an issue. The current information and resources available on animals, however, is more suitable for primary students.

The core of the unit involves students investigating one particular animal and then sharing and comparing the information gathered with others.

The unit employs the term 'threatened' throughout although it encourages students to eventually understand the difference between the terms 'threatened', 'endangered' and 'extinct'.

Understandings

- Humans and other animals co-exist on this planet.
- Extinction is a natural process. However, since the evolution of humans the rate of extinction has increased rapidly.
- The extinction of plants and animals, particularly those at the base of the food chain, has direct consequences for all life forms, including humans.
- When a species of animal or plant is at risk, other animals and plants that depend on it are also likely to be at risk.
- There are various causes of endangerment. These include habitat loss, hunting, and destruction by feral animals.
- There are ways that people can help protect threatened species.

Key concepts

Extinction	Cause and effect
Threats	Native and feral
Needs vs wants	Interdependence
Habitat	Survival

Skills

Values clarification	Debating and presenting an argument
Classification	Gathering and interpreting data
Problem solving	Empathising
Deduction and clear thinking	Co-operating

"ON BEHALF OF OTHER ANIMALS"—SAMPLE UNIT PLANNER

		Session 1	Session 2	Session 3	Session 4	Session 5	Ongoing Activities
Tuning In ↓ Preparing to find out	Week 1	TUNING IN · What's it like to be endanger · Book: The Wump World	· Making plans for classroom pet - designing Suitable habitat	· Selecting design Preparing enclosure · Needs - Rules for Care	PREPARING TO FIND OUT · Causes of endangerment (Groups) BLM1	· Class Listing - Causes	· Roster & Routine to care for pet.
↓ Finding Out	Week 2	· Animal allocation Yes/No game Pre Zoo prediction	· Visit to Zoo - threatened animals BLM2	· Visit to Zoo - threatened animals.	· Visit to Zoo - threatened Animals	SORTING OUT Art · Making Masks	· Monitor classroom pet. Daily diary observations etc.
↓ Sorting Out	Week 3	Art · Creating habitat corners in the room.	Movement - Animals moves Using masks	Language · Revise understandings · Model report	· Report writing on individual animals	· Class Book making	Build up list of threatened animals. Data base
↓ Going Further	Week 4	· Information chart - patterns BLM3	Maths · Survey of statistical info. about animals	· Visual representation of statistics	Drama · Moral dilemmas Values Clarification BLM 4	Movement · Animal moves	
↓ Making Connections	Week 5	· Statements from Maps	GOING FURTHER · Laying it on the line BLMS	· Sharing Circle	· Sharing Circle	MAKING CONNECTIONS Concept mappings	Use statements for language activities.
↓ Taking Action	Week 6	TAKING ACTION · Revise what we have learned.	· Considering action.	· Implementing action	· Implementing action.	· Reflecting on Unit	

Tuning in

The activities suggested here are designed simply to get students engaged in thinking about the topic. They are designed to sensitise and motivate students . . . to 'get the ball rolling.'

Literature is often a useful starting point and suggestions are offered in the resources list near the end of the unit.

In danger

Discuss these questions:

- What does 'threatened' mean? Brainstorm reactions to this focus question.
- When have you been in danger? How did you feel?

(Small groups sit together and share their personal experience of danger. They make a list of elements common to these experiences.)

> You feel like you're out of control
> You wish that there was someone else to help you.
> You feel like crying. You're scared of being hurt.
> You feel like screaming. You feel sick.
> You can be too scared to speak.
> You can often be in a strange place —you wish that you were at home or with your family.

As this discussion can lead to some sensitive revelations, it is most important to bring students together and talk about the way that they get out of danger and then to make a collective list about those.

> Someone comes to help you.
> You make a loud noise.
> You run away.
> You talk to yourself and calm yourself down.
> You pretend that you're not scared.
> You think of a way to get out of the situation.
> Nothing happens— it was a false alarm.

The purpose of the activity above is to provide a basis for the development of empathy. Although animals may not share the feelings and thought processes of humans in danger, they have similar ways of expressing fear and this is not always recognised by people as fear but is often seen as aggression.

Ask the students how they think this exercise relates to the endangerment of animals. They are not always directly threatened in the ways discussed above. Discuss the following:

- In what ways are humans less directly threatened? (sickness, poverty, etc.)
- In what ways are animals less directly threatened? (pollution, decreasing habitat, disease)

Animals in the classroom

Another suggested activity to begin to develop students' empathy and to add a valuable dimension to the unit is to organise an animal to be kept in the classroom for a short period.

There are various opinions about the value of this for students. Some may argue that it gives students the wrong messages about keeping animals in captivity etc. In the author's experience however, it is extremely valuable for students and, if handled well, can be a useful way of demonstrating the needs that animals have and how they are met.

There are animals that are more appropriate for classrooms (e.g. guinea pigs) and many that are not allowed to be kept at all. You are advised to contact the education department in your state to get a list of acceptable species and guidelines for keeping them in captivity.

Designing a habitat

Students should be involved as much as possible in designing an environment that meets the animal's needs. As a class, decide on what those needs are. Consider such factors as safety, warmth, protection, food, water, care. How will we meet the animal's needs?

Throughout the time that the classroom pet is with you, talk about the needs it has in comparison to the animals you are finding out about, and in comparison with humans.

Human needs	How are they met?	Guinea pig's needs	How are they met?
Warmth	Clothes, housing heating	warmth	fur, cage
food	buy food grown from plants or from animals	food	we feed him lettuce and pellets

Records of the animal's growth, habits, food preferences, movements etc. may be kept through a class diary or on charts.

Preparing to find out

These activities are designed with three main aims:
1. To give you some insight into what the students already know about the topic and where their initial interests lie;
2. To help students focus clearly on what they already know and what they will try to find out. Some activities require the students to make decisions about the ways they will go about gathering information;
3. To prepare the students for the experience to follow (e.g. an excursion) and to focus their investigations.

Introducing five threatened animals

| Eastern barred bandicoot |

| Dugong |

| Eltham copper butterfly |

| Pouched frog |

| Palm cockatoo |

Divide the grade into five groups.

Present each group with a picture of a threatened animal and a short description of it. (BLMs 1–5, pages 172–176 can be used for this.)

Students discuss the animal and list all their ideas about why that animal is now threatened. What things might have put it in danger? Share lists as a grade and make a collective one. Can the list be classified in any way?

> feral and domestic animals
> clearing land
> hunting for food
> hunting for luxury items
> illegal trade
> pollution
> predators
> loss of food source
> disease / natural disaster

One way to categorise the items is to ask which causes are natural and which are a result of human activity? Return to groups and use reference materials to clarify and modify lists. Report to class.

After the reports, ask, 'Can we add to the list?'

As a brainstorming activity, the class lists animals they think are extinct, endangered and not threatened. At this stage, accept all suggestions. The list can be modified during the unit.

Add to the list with the assistance of the material in the reference list at the end of the unit.

Discuss the question, 'How can we find out more about threatened animals?' with students and list some of the means by which you can gather further information about the topic.

Finding out

These experiences are designed to give students the opportunity to gather new information about the topic.

A visit to the zoo

There is nothing quite like the direct experience of seeing animals, albeit in an artificial setting. A visit to the zoo or wildlife sanctuary is suggested as a shared experience for this unit. You need to ensure that there are, in fact, endangered animals on display and that you have some information about them beforehand.

Many zoos offer a trail through enclosures displaying various threatened species. One example is the 'Conservation Safari' at Taronga Zoo in Sydney. Try to see a range of animal types, including birds, reptiles, insects, small and large mammals, amphibians and fish. It would be useful to arrange a talk or lesson from a staff member at the zoo on a threatened species topic such as a captive breeding program — something many zoos are now undertaking.

If a visit to the zoo is not possible, there are a range of books, videos and organisations that could provide students with information to work with. Examples of these less direct experiences are listed below:

- *Let's not Say Goodbye* TV Education video-tape available from various state education department media dubbing services.
- Slides of endangered animals and a sound tape to go with them — available from the Melbourne Zoo.

Also, organisations such as those in the 'useful addresses section' of the resource list at the end of the unit will be able to offer advice on other suitable material.

Animal guardians

Before visiting the zoo, ask for a list of threatened species there.

Use the game 'Yes/No' to allocate a particular animal to a student or small group of students. To do this, pin the name and picture (if available) of a threatened animal at the zoo to each student's back. They then wander around the room asking questions about their animal requiring a yes/no answer only. When they have guessed the animal (they need only to guess the type of animal, not the actual specific name), they remove the name and put it on their chest.

Tell them then that the animals they have are all threatened in some way. At the zoo, that will be their special animal to find out about. They will become the guardian of that animal.

At the zoo, allow students to visit the enclosure where their animal is housed. It would be best for them to be in small groups with a parent per group, perhaps organised so that they will be visiting similar areas of the zoo.

Allow time for students to take down information about their animal, to photograph it, to sketch it, to watch the way it moves, to note the things in its environment etc. The BLM 2 on page 177 could be used to assist in gathering information.

Predictions — thaumatropes

In pairs or as individuals, students make a list of the things they know and would like to know about their special animal (identified in the activity above).

Students draw the animal in the habitat that they think it will be in: in the wild; and in the zoo. Students then use the references in the resource list at the end of the units to check the accuracy of the habitats they have drawn.

A fun activity is to make 'thaumatropes'. On a small piece of card, draw the habitat. On the other side of the card, draw the animal. Attach string to both ends, twist it, then pull. The card spins around as the string unravels. The animal will appear to be 'in' the habitat.

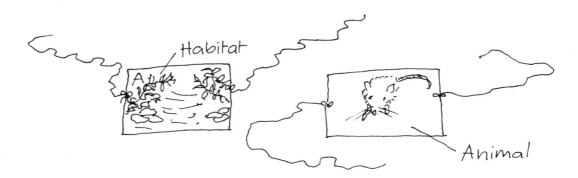

Sorting out

At this stage a variety of activities is suggested across a range of curriculum areas. Students will process information they have gathered and present it in a number of different ways. They may also begin to draw some conclusions about what it is they have learnt.

Art

Initial responses to the shared experiences can be represented through a variety of art activities. Provide students with a range of materials with which they can represent their experience. Suggestions are to be found below:

A special home

Use the art materials to represent the habitat that your animal lives in. Compare it to another habitat or to that animal's true, natural habitat.

Giant zoo map

Create a giant map of the zoo with the various endangered species painted at the appropriate site. Label the mural with facts about those animals.

Making models

Make a model of your particular animal in its habitat. Create a 3-D class diorama.

Portraits

Use the sketches and photos of the animals to make some detailed line drawings of the animals. Mount them on coloured card and display them.

Habitat corners

Students work in groups according to the habitat that their animal lives in (e.g. rainforests, deserts, wetlands, trees). Groups use a variety of art materials to represent that habitat in one area of the room.

Masks

This is a highly recommended follow-up activity to the zoo visit. It may be something that the students could do during their specialist art time. Students construct a face mask of their special animal. They will need to use books, photos and their imaginations to do so. These masks will be used in movement activities and in the final, reflective sharing circle.

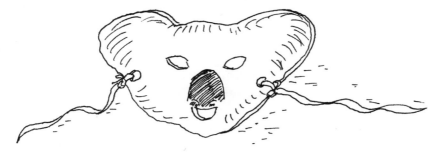

Food chains

Students use the information they have gathered and the resources around the room to work out where their particular animal fits into a food chain. They should begin by finding out what it eats and then what eats it!

Mobiles can be made illustrating the links between their animal and other animals and plants.

What would happen to the animals in the chain if your animal became extinct?

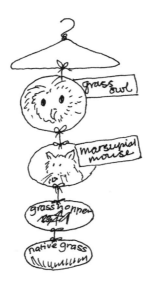

Language

Revisiting

Return to the original predictions about different animals. What information can students add and change?

Text analysis and report writing

This activity is designed to complete the individual animal study and give each student the opportunity to inform others about what he or she knows. Choose one threatened animal that students saw at the zoo and one on which you have some written information, e.g. mountain gorillas. The resource list near the end of this unit has many books that would make suitable models.

In groups, students brainstorm all they know about gorillas

Read to the whole a class factual text about gorillas, e.g. from Vincent Serventy's book, *Animals in Danger*. Ask students the questions: 'What information did the author include about this animal? What could you add to your notes on gorillas?' Return to the results of their brainstorming (above) and refine the information gathered.

The teacher then models the construction of a report on gorillas using the group's information and the model presented in the factual text. Some areas to cover are the type of animal, where it is found, its appearance, its needs, its habitat, its food and the threats to its survival.

Students now use the information they have gathered about their own animals to construct a report. If they have been working in pairs, they can conference each other. If they are working individually, they should be encouraged to team up with others and to talk about their plans. The report could be as simple or complex as you wish — it may accompany photos taken at the zoo or portraits made.

Reports could be compiled into a large, class book and read to other classes.

Information chart

When reports are finalised, a class retrieval chart could be developed on which to show collected data. This is important as students will begin to see patterns emerging. A sample chart is provided on BLM 3. This could be filled in by groups of students prior to the development of a large class chart. The chart will include information about animals in relation to their country of origin, appearance, food, habitat, threats and protective devices.

Maths

Visual representation

A variety of visual representation activities could be done based on the information gathered at the zoo. For example, students may list all the animals seen and classify them into groups. This is represented on a chart.

By pooling and comparing information, students will be able to draw some conclusions about common characteristics of endangered species and about common threats to survival.

Using a database

Programs such as Apple Works enable students to develop their own database using the information they have gathered. This is an excellent way of organising and storing information and could be added to throughout the unit.

A database on threatened mammals is available for use in schools and would be a good model of this way of organising and storing information. (See resource list near the end of the unit for details.)

Surveys

In small groups, students nominate different aspects of the threatened species to survey the whole class about and then graph the results. Below are some aspects to present to students:

- Find out the numbers left in the wild and visually represent this.
- Find out the foods that each animal needs and visually represent this.
- Find out where the animal originates from and represent this on a map.
- Find out the major threat to each animal and show this on a graph.

Use the following activity to introduce or practise percentages or fractions.

- What percentage of our animals have been hunted for food?
- What percentage of our animals are forest dwellers?
- What percentage of our animals are Australian?

Use BLM 7 p. 182 to help students develop their surveys and graphs.

Some further maths activities that would assist students in understanding the nature of species loss would be ones where they try to graph or represent some of the alarming statistics that are documented in most of the literature available on the subject. They will also notice enormous variations between statistics on the same animals. Discuss why this happens.

Drama

Moral dilemma

The moral dilemma activity using BLM 5 is designed to give students an insight into the complexities that arise out of the threatened species issue. It is easy to say that we must simply stop killing or destroying habitat but the reality is that many people's livelihoods have depended on these very actions. Secondly, we are not always certain of the way our actions affect species. (Two dilemmas have been provided. Once students have got the hang of it they could design their own to present to the grade.)

Divide students into groups of three. One person is the decision-maker. The others are the 'for' and 'against' voices of his/her conscience.

It is best to demonstrate the activity first with the assistance of two students. Read the moral dilemma to the grade or have students read it in their groups.

The 'consciences' stand either side of the decision-maker and alternately put their point of view across. They speak as the voice of the decision-maker and take it in turns to put across an argument. Below is an example of students arguing in role:

Give the students a set time to go through the debate. The decision-maker must then decide what to do. The decision-makers then share their decision with the group and explain why they were convinced.

Variations on the dilemmas

The moral dilemma could also be used as the basis of mini-plays that the students act out to show various ways of handling the same situation.

The moral dilemmas could be approached from a variety of perspectives, according to the various viewpoints of the people involved in them, for example, in 'Burgers or Buddies', the point of view of one of the other kids at the party. In 'Buildings or Butterflies,' the point of view of the builder who has been hired to do the work.

Talking about it

It is important to spend some time debriefing after these activities. Ask the students why they made the decisions they made. Ask them:

- What sort of arguments were effective?
- How did you feel?
- What are some good strategies for sorting out our problems?
- What things influence our decision-making?

Movement

Animal moves

Do some warm-up exercises. If you are in a big space let students run around initially to let off steam.

Ask students to close their eyes and think again about their special animal. Think, in particular, about the way it moved.

- What shape is it? Can you make that shape with your body? Find your own moving space.
- Where does it move? Close to the ground? Up and down? In a tree?
- Is it fast or slow or varied? Try out some ways of moving.
- Does it have a preferred position when it is still?

Students think about the way their particular animal moved at various times of day. Become your animal looking for food. Become your animal dozing in the sun. Become your animal frightened or in danger.

- Team up animals that move in similar ways. Together, form a sequence of three movements.
- Team up animals that would be found in the same habitat. Develop a sequence where the animals meet and interact.

Use a drum or tambour to beat out a rhythm as students move around. This will help keep them focussed.

Warm down with some relaxation exercises. The movement activities can allow for a very different expression of understanding about the animals that the students have seen. It is important that the session be well structured and organised and the rules for behaviour are known. Masks or props can often diffuse inhibitions.

Going further

These activities are designed to challenge and extend students' understandings of the topic.

Laying it on the line

This activity can be done either by individuals or as a whole grade. If you take the latter course, you will need a length of string. Attach a card to each end: one reads 'strongly agree' the other 'strongly disagree'.

As you or a student reads out the statements on BLM 6, students must place themselves along the string according to how they feel about each one. At the end of the activity, you should discuss the way they felt and the things that influenced their decision-making.

Again, students could use this approach with statements generated by themselves.

Sharing circle

A good prop for this activity is the mask that students may have made when they returned from the zoo. This will help students get into role quickly and feel less inhibited about sharing.

This activity is designed to develop students' empathy for other living things and to encourage them to question the role of humans as a power over other living things. It is best done in an outdoor, natural setting and needs about half an hour.

Step 1 When children are outside ask them to sit in a circle and close their eyes. They are to imagine that they have become a plant or animal that is threatened by the activities of humans. They should think about why they are an important part of the ecosystem and what makes them special. They may decide to adopt the role of the animal for which they were a guardian before and after the zoo.

Step 2 Ask someone who is ready to enter the middle of the circle. The others represent all humankind. Basically, the student in the middle has the opportunity to speak for that animal as it cannot speak for itself. The student begins by announcing, 'I speak for the bandicoots.'

Step 3 The teacher could begin by modelling some questions from the humans, e.g. 'Tell us about yourself bandicoot. Where do you live? Why are you special? The student in the middle spends some time telling the humans about the animal it represents. The humans have the chance to ask it questions.

Step 4 Teacher then asks the animal, 'What troubles you bandicoot?

The bandicoot tells the humans of its plight and may ask them questions: 'Why have you let your cats free to chase and kill us? Why have you taken away the things we like to eat?' The humans listen and respond if they wish. The teacher asks, 'Who else would like to speak on behalf of something that is threatened?' Another student enters the circle when he or she is ready to speak on behalf of a threatened species. (It may be the special animal that he or she has studied throughout the unit.) Students only enter the circle if they feel confident to do so.

Afterwards, talk about the way students felt as the animal and as the humans.

Making connections

At this stage, students will be drawing conclusions about what they have learnt. This is an important time for you to evaluate the success of the unit and the needs and achievements of individuals. This is where students 'put it all together'.

Concept mapping

Present students with the following key words:

- animals
- habitat
- food chain
- threatened
- extinct
- humans
- hunting
- clearing
- feral animals
- habitat
- survival
- wants

Students organise them on a large sheet in a way that makes sense to them.

Animals plants   threatened   Habitat
Food chain
Survival   clearing
hunting
Extinct   wants
Humans

They then draw some connecting lines between words and indicate how they believe their words relate to each other.

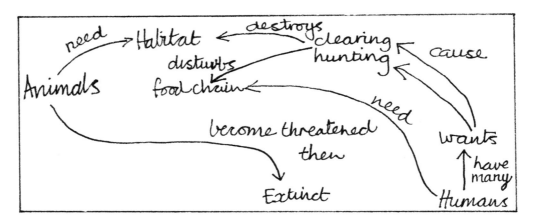

This forms a concept map.

From their maps, students come up with one statement about threatened species. They then meet in groups and share maps and statements.

Each group writes a list of statements agreed upon by their group. They try to put them into some sort of priority order.

The "wants" of humans can cause habitat destruction for animals.

Animals can become threatened if their food chain is destroyed.

The survival of many animals depends on humans.

They share statements with the whole grade and ask themselves, 'What statements belong together? Does everybody agree? What questions do we have?'

Related language activities

- Cut the statements up and re-sequence them.
- Use the statements as the basis for a cloze activity.
- Underline words that have common structures (e.g. similar sounds or letter patterns).
- Look at the different types of words in the statements, e.g. nouns, adjectives, verbs.
- Classify the statements that are about similar ideas.

Use these statements and concept maps to evaluate students' understandings.

Taking action

This is a very important element of both the inquiry process and of environmental education. It is essential that students be given opportunities to act upon what they have learnt.

Suggestions for personal and class action

Students should have the opportunity now to suggest some form of personal or collective action on the basis of what they have learnt.

As a class you may decide on things that you could do together and things that you could do in small groups or as individuals. The following are some suggestions that relate to this topic:

- Join an organisation that protects threatened species, e.g. World Wildlife Fund for Nature.
- Sponsor an endangered or threatened animal at the zoo.
- Write letters to companies or politicians expressing concern for activities that threaten species.
- Run a school campaign on the correct restraint of domestic pets, e.g. bells on cats, lock animals inside at night time.
- Let other people in the school or community know what you have learnt about threatened species. This could be done by inviting people in to view the various pieces of work that have been created throughout the unit.

- Plant native trees in the school yard to attract more native bird-life.
- Avoid buying wildlife or wildlife products.

Resources

Books for children
Baker, Jeannie *Where the Forest Meets the Sea* Macrae 1988
Burton, Robert *Wildlife in Danger* Macmillan 1981
Coleridge, A. *Stranded* Five Mile Press
Haddon, F. and Oliver, T. *The Gould League Book of Australian Endangered Wildlife* Gould League 1983
Herve, A. *Animal Man* Harlin Quist 1976
Howes, J. *Skin, Scales, Feathers and Fur* Macmillan 1987
Mendoza, G. *The Hunter I Might Have Been* Ten Speed Press 1968
Peet, B. *The Wump World* Houghton Mifflin 1970
Serventy, Vincent *Animals in Danger* John Ferguson 1989
Serventy, V. and Carnegie, M. *Wildlife of the Australian Bush* Ellsyd Press 1985
Thiele, Colin *The Sknuks* (Opal Books) Rigby 1977
Wagner, J. *The Bunyip of Berkley's Creek* Puffin 1973

Teaching resources
Creagh, C. and Atkinson, K. *The Ones That Got Away* Methuen 1986
Feral Animals Gould League
Feral Peril: Activities to Help Form Values about Wildlife Conservation Gould League 1990
Howes, J. *The Edge of Extinction* Gould League
Outdoor Environmental Games Gould League
Riordan, D. and Peterson, K. *Springboards: Ideas for Animal Studies* Nelson

General books on endangered animals
Attenborough, D. *Life on Earth* Collins 1979
The Living Planet Collins 1979
Australian Broadcasting Corporation *Nature of Australia* Collins (also available on video)
Kennedy, M. (ed.) *A Complete Reference to Australia's Endangered Species* Simon and Schuster 1990 (includes plants and animals)
Ovington, D. *Australian Endangered Species: Mammals, Birds and Reptiles* Cassell 1978
Vanishing Species Time Life Books 1990

Useful addresses
Australian Conservation Foundation
340 Gore Street
Fitzroy
Vic. 3065

Australian National Parks and Wildlife Services
PO Box 636 (Endangered Species Unit)
Canberra
ACT 2601

Film and Video Collection
117 Bouverie Street
Carlton
Tel. (03) 342 3911

Film and Video Library
3 Small Road
Ryde
NSW 2112
Tel. (02) 808 9521

Fund for Animals
GPO Box 371
Manly
NSW
Tel. (02) 977 1912

National Threatened Species Network
Coordinator based at World Wide Fund for Nature
247 Flinders Lane
Melbourne 3000 Tel. (03) 650 7011

Database
Goodbye Forever: A Database of Threatened Mammals for Apple II
computers; available from the Hawthorn Institute of Education, 442 Auburn
Road, Hawthorn, Vic. 3122. Tel. (03) 810 3322

Introducing threatened animals

The eastern barred bandicoot.

This is a small, nocturnal marsupial — it is a little smaller than a rabbit with a long, pointed nose. The bandicoot has soft, brown fur with a creamy-coloured belly, feet and tail. It has a series of 'stripes' on its back that give it its name — a barred bandicoot. Its natural habitat is woodland and grassland but these days many of them can be found in the junk in an old rubbish tip in Western Victoria. They live very close to a town.

Why do you think that this bandicoot might be threatened?

✂ — ✂

For the teacher

The eastern barred bandicoot is a very rapid breeder. Up to five young can be produced every sixteen days — this is the shortest gestation period for any marsupial. Despite this, the main population is currently only about 300 animals and getting smaller. The reason behind its decline is, predominantly, killing by domestic cats. Native habitat has virtually been eliminated from around the town of Hamilton where it is found. This land was cleared for farming.

Introducing threatened animals

The pouched frog

Like many other frogs, this small brown frog is threatened. The pouched frog gets its name from the male which incubates the young in two pouches — one on either side of its body! It is found only around the border between New South Wales and Queensland and lives under rocks and rotting logs in rainforests. It needs moist conditions to survive.

Why do you think this frog is threatened?

✂ — ✂

For the teacher

There are two main reasons for the decline in numbers of this species of frog: it lives in a very restricted range and its rainforest habitat is under threat of logging.

Many scientists believe that the disappearance of frogs across the world may be due to their vulnerability to increasing water pollution.

Introducing threatened animals

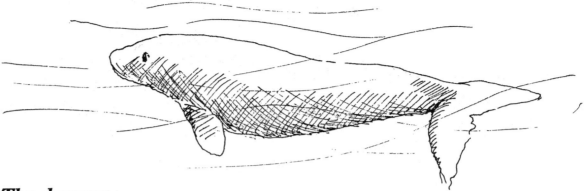

The dugong

This large, gentle sea mammal is the only plant-eating mammal that lives only in the sea. The dugong likes to swim in warm, shallow waters and needs lots of healthy seagrass to feed on. It can be found near beaches which are protected from sharks by large nets. It is sometimes hunted for food.

　　Why do you think the dugong is threatened?

✂ — ✂

For the teacher

The major threats to dugongs are from direct hunting (although they are now protected in Australian waters). They are also killed in nets designed to catch sharks, and fishing nets. In the long term, the destruction of coastal habitat and pollution pose the biggest threats.

Introducing threatened animals

The Eltham copper butterfly

This beautiful and delicate, copper-coloured butterfly is found in only a few places in Victoria. It lays its eggs on one kind of plant only. When the caterpillars hatch they are fed by ants who, in turn, use a substance made by the caterpillar to build their nest.

Why do you think this butterfly is threatened?

✂ — ✂

For the teacher

The Eltham copper butterfly is found in fewer than half a dozen locations within Victoria. Most of these are close to urban areas, where the threat of housing development is ever-present. Because of its curious life cycle — it depends on an ant and a particular species of plant (Bursaria) — the Eltham copper butterfly has a very rare habitat. It is therefore very vulnerable to land development.

Introducing threatened animals

The palm cockatoo

The palm cockatoo gets its name from its favourite food — the seeds of a palm. It is dark grey with a red patch on its cheek. Its huge beak is used to crack open nuts and seeds. Palm cockatoos are found only in the very top corner of Australia — near Cape York, where they live between thick rainforest and dry forest. There are very few of these beautiful birds in captivity.

Why do you think this cockatoo is threatened?

✂ — ✂

For the teacher

The palm cockatoo, like many Australian birds, is affected by threats from bird traders. Its rarity and its exquisite beauty make it particularly vulnerable to smuggling and transportation overseas. Naturally, many birds do not survive the journey and the wild population is further depleted. Recently, reports that a space port will be built near Cape York have added further to the threats facing this bird.

At the zoo

Use this sheet to take notes about your special threatened animal. Spend some time watching and listening . . . *really* watching and listening . . .

Animal name_____ My name_____

Appearance
What does your animal look like? Write down its colours, special features, covering, etc. Make a quick sketch of it.

_____

_____

_____

_____

Movement
How does your animal move? Watch it for a while and write down some words that describe the movements it makes. Does it make a noise?

_____

_____

_____

Habitat
What sort of habitat is the animal in? Draw the enclosure and label the important parts of it. Can you see where the animal might sleep? Can you see where it can hide? What seems to be its favourite spot in the enclosure? Mark the places that the animal uses.

_____

_____

_____

_____

Country
Can you find out where the animal comes from? What information about it is displayed?

_____

_____

Food
Can you see what the animal eats?

_____

(Use the back of the page to write down any other interesting things you notice about your animal.)

Threatened species information chart

Use the information that you have gathered about threatened species to fill in this chart. What patterns do you notice? What conclusions can you draw?

Animal and Country	Description	Habitat	Food	Threats	Protective Devices
Numbat Australia	Small marsupial, brown with white stripes	woodlands — forest floor hollow logs or ground burrow	insects — especially termites	Foxes and feral cats, birds of prey. Clearing of woodland.	Camouflage.

Threatened Animals Survey

Before the Survey . . .

Who are the people in the group? List the names below.

_____

What is your survey about?

_____

_____

How will you gather information from the other children in the class?

_____

_____

What do you think the results will be?

_____

_____

_____

_____

After the Survey . . .

How will you represent your results to others? (Think about the different sorts of graphs that you could use.)

_____

_____

_____

_____

What materials do you need?

_____

_____

_____

What conclusions can you draw about threatened species from looking at your graph?

_____

_____

_____

_____

Moral dilemmas

Buildings or Butterflies?

After working hard and saving money for many years, you recently bought a block of bush-land on which you are planning to build a house. You love the bush and have wanted to live away from the city for a long time. Until now, everything has been going really well. You have just got a job in the nearby town and you have resigned from your old job in the city. You have designed your energy-efficient house, hired builders and purchased the materials. Your elderly mother will be coming to live with you in this house. She suffers from asthma and the doctors say that the clean country air will do her good.

You have just been told, however, by a local conservation organisation that a small population of the rare golden butterfly has been discovered on the very site you plan to build your house. It had been thought that only two populations of these exist in the world. The butterfly population has an important relationship with the plants that grow on your block. It pollinates them and, in turn, those plants grow to feed a range of other living things.

You are told that any disturbance to the butterfly's habitat will put their survival at great risk. What's more, the council has said that they will not buy the land from you. What will you do?

Burgers or Buddies

Your family recently decided that they would no longer eat hamburgers. This decision was made after you had watched a TV program about the destruction of rainforests. You learnt that the destruction of rainforest overseas was sometimes due to the clearing of land to graze cattle for meat. When rainforest is destroyed, *many* rare plants and animals are threatened. You all agreed that you would boycott all hamburger shops as a protest against this clearance. Not only is the meat in the hamburgers environmentally unsound but so are all the disposable plates, napkins, cutlery and containers. You know that many important animal and plant species depend on the rainforest for their survival.

You have also recently started at a new school. Things haven't been going all that well for you — it's been difficult to make new friends and you have been feeling pretty lonely and miserable. Some of the kids have been giving you a hard time because you're not allowed out after school very often.

To your surprise and delight, one of the coolest kids in the grade asks you to a party. Many of the kids in the grade are going. Amazingly, your mum and dad say it's OK — they give you some spending money, and encourage you to have a great time. At last . . . you have a chance to make some friends and show the other kids that you are worth knowing! Excitedly, you hurry off to meet them after school. But wouldn't you know it . . . ! The party is being held at a hamburger restaurant . . . the very one whose products you have made a pact to boycott. The others are about to go in . . . what will you do?

Laying it on the line

What do you think about these statements? Mark the spot on the line to show where you stand. Remember . . . there are no right or wrong answers.

We should keep more animals in zoos to protect them from extinction.

strongly agree •————————————————————————————• strongly disagree

It is more important to protect endangered mammals than endangered insects.

strongly agree •————————————————————————————• strongly disagree

It is more important to protect animals than plants.

strongly agree •————————————————————————————• strongly disagree

All animals have the same right to live as human beings.

strongly agree •————————————————————————————• strongly disagree

If a shark is seen in an area where people like to swim, it should be killed.

strongly agree •————————————————————————————• strongly disagree

We should try to protect our Australian animals before we worry about other countries' animals.

strongly agree •————————————————————————————• strongly disagree

Lots of animals have disappeared from the Earth already. Extinction is natural — we shouldn't waste our time trying to stop it.

strongly agree •————————————————————————————• strongly disagree

All dogs and cats should be tied up or kept inside to protect native animals.

strongly agree •————————————————————————————• strongly disagree

All hunting should be banned.

strongly agree •————————————————————————————• strongly disagree

Some threatened animals of Australia

Albert's lyrebird
Baw Baw frog
Boyd's forest dragon
bush thicknee
carpet snake
dugong
eastern barred bandicoot
giant Gippsland earthworm
Gouldian finch
great white shark
green turtle
honey possum
magpie goose
mountain pygmy possum

musky rat-kangaroo
numbat
orange-bellied parrot
palm cockatoo
peregrine falcon
pig-nosed turtle
red kangaroo
ring-tailed gecko
western quail
yellow-bellied glider
yellow-tailed black cockatoo
helmeted honey eater
northern hairy-nosed wombat
Eltham copper butterfly

Planning your own units of work

This section is designed to assist you in planning your own units of work based on the format that has been used in this book. **This should be useful not only in the area of environmental education but in the other content areas of science, social studies and personal development.** There are many ways to plan for an integrated curriculum — this is only one. You should modify it to suit your own style, circumstances and needs of your students.

Whatever format you use to design your own units, it is important that basic principles of integrated curriculum remain. Working through the following questions may assist you in doing this:

- Have I provided students with opportunities to work in a range of grouping situations?
- Have I provided students with some opportunities to work co-operatively with each other?
- Does my planning accommodate a range of needs and abilities? Are there open-ended tasks that students could approach at a variety of levels?
- Does my planning allow students to make some choices about what they will do?
- Does my planning provide structure and sequence so that both the students and I know where we are heading and why?
- Have I incorporated a range of curriculum areas so that students will have the opportunity to process information in a variety of ways?
- Have I provided opportunities for students to self-evaluate and reflect on what they have learned? Good Luck!

Unit planning sheet

Term:

Topic:

Approx. duration:

Focus curriculum area:

Understandings

Key Concepts

Skills

Tuning in ... activities to engage students in the topic.

Planning your own units of work

Preparing to find out ... activities that give insight into what students already know and that prepare them for further investigations.

Finding out ... a shared experience from which students will gather new information about the topic.

Sorting out... activities that help students process the information that they have gathered.

Main curriculum areas used:

Planning your own units of work

Going Further... activities that challenge and extend students' understandings.

Making Connections... activities that help students put it all together and draw some conclusions about what they have learnt.

Taking Action ... activities that give students the opportunity to act upon what they have learnt.

Planning an integrated unit . . . some questions to ask yourself

Choosing a topic
- Is this topic meaningful?
- Is it worth doing? Will it lead students to new understandings about the way their world works?
- Is it relevant to their lives in some way?
- Does it fit in with our school program?

Gathering resources
- What has already been produced in this area? What materials are available to us?
- Do we need to do any reading about the topic?
- Do we know any experts in the area?

Writing understandings
- What do we hope students will understand about their social or physical world by the end of this unit? What is important and relevant for these students?

Tuning in
- How can we *engage* students in this topic?
- What media can we use ?
- How can we get them thinking and talking about it?

Preparing to find out
- How can we assess students' prior knowledge?
- How can we involve them in negotiating the direction of the unit? What should they do prior to the shared experience?

Finding out
- What experience/s can we organise that will enable students to gather new information about the topic?
- How can we help *focus* their investigations?

Sorting out
How can we use the various process areas of the curriculum to help students sort out their data?
— Art
— Drama
— Maths
— Music
— Movement
— Language

Going further
- How can we further students' experience and understanding about this topic?
- How can we challenge their ideas and give them new perspectives? How can they process this new information?

Making connections
- How can we assist students in pulling it all together?
- What curriculum processes would help here? Language, drama, art . . . ?
- How can we see if they are making connections?

Taking action
- How can we empower students to act on what they have learnt?
- What might be some appropriate forms of action?

Comments:

UNIT PLANNER

	Session 1	Session 2	Session 3	Session 4	Session 5	Ongoing Activities
Tuning in → Preparing to find out Week 1						
Finding out Week 2						
Sorting out Week 3						
Going Further Week 4						
Making Connections → Week 5						
Taking Action Week 6						

Setting up your classroom for an integrated curriculum

Our class curriculum includes all the arrangements that we make for students' learning. An integrated curriculum is made easier to teach if your classroom has appropriate and accessible materials and is well organised. Below are some suggested ways of organising your room that will facilitate the teaching of these units.

Classrooms certainly come in all shapes and sizes and it is not always possible to set them up in a ways that suits us best. There are, however, some important features that should be included:

- *Some tables in groups.* As there are many times throughout the units where students work in groups, it is important that there are some tables that are positioned in a way that makes this possible.
- *Some individual tables.* There are also times when some students will need or choose to work on their own. Your classroom should have some individual, 'quiet' tables for this to occur.
- *Writing and publishing materials.* An area should be set aside for the storage of writing materials, including pens, textas, pencils and various sizes and types of paper and card. These materials should be available to students rather than locked in a cupboard. Students themselves can be given the responsibility for monitoring the 'use and abuse' of materials.
- *An area for displays about the current topic.* A part of the room should be left available to set up 'learning centres' for each unit. This is a place where experiments, books, games etc. can be accessed by the students as part of their ongoing learning.
- *A meeting area.* A place should be set aside where you can meet together as a class. This does not have to be in front of the board! It should be somewhere that is comfortable.
- *Personal space for each student.* Throughout these integrated units, students are required to share and co-operate with each other. It is important, however, that they have an area in the room that they consider theirs — where they can store work, belongings etc. Rather than a set table (which makes it difficult to use a range of grouping strategies) this may be a locker, tub or book bag.

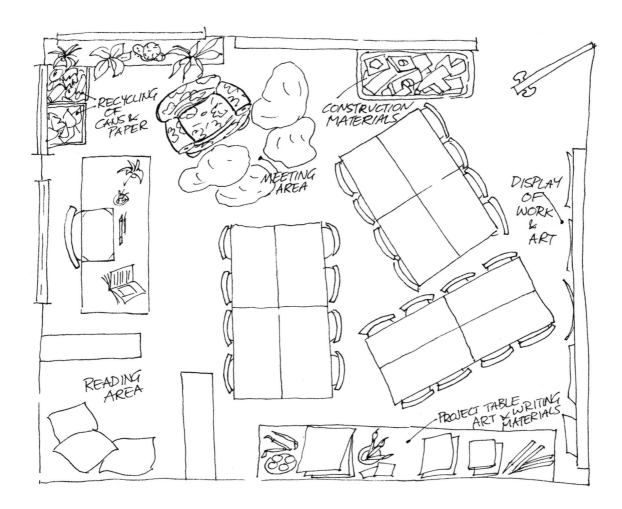

Often, as students move into the upper grades, fewer resources become available to them, e.g. art and construction materials. For an integrated curriculum to run effectively, it is important that all students have access to a range of materials that will help them investigate, process and represent their learning in a variety of ways.

It is surprising how often much of this material is in fact *in* schools — it is however, either under lock and key or left to gather dust in a forgotten cupboard.

The following section lists some of the materials that are used regularly by teachers who work in an integrated way. The material should be stored such a way that it is accessible to teachers and students alike. Some of it will need to be shared between grades. The important thing is that students know where it is and are aware of the rules for its use. Given the responsibility for the materials, they will soon learn about the importance of sharing and caring for it. Also, once students are able to access their own materials, you are less likely to spend too much time 'handing out and gathering up' at the beginning and end of sessions.

Classroom materials for an integrated curriculum — middle to upper primary

Art materials

paint
crayons or pastels
textas (thick and thin)
coloured pencils
brushes and rollers
coloured paper
infant squares
material scraps
magazines
soft modelling wire
masking tape
paste
PVA glue

wool
string
plasticine or playdough
newspapers
scissors
Stanley knife
staplers
cellophane
crepe or tissue paper
sticky labels
drawing pins
paper clips
sponges
bucket

Art and cleaning materials should be non-toxic. Students could make up their own environmentally safe cleaner. A useful resource for this is Barbara Lord's book, *The Green Cleaner*, ACF and S&W Books, 1989.

Construction and maths materials

Lego
Unifix or Multi-link
straws
wood off-cuts
stencils for shapes

rulers
trundle wheel
tape measures
calculators
cardboard

Reference materials

Range of factual texts (can be changed according to current topic)
dictionaries

picture story books and novels
telephone book
photo albums for class photos during units

thesaurus
encyclopaedia
magazines (e.g. *Comet, Habitat, Australian Geo, National Geographic*)
newspapers

street directory for local area
map of the world or atlas
map of Australia

Writing and publishing materials

pens
pencils
textas
rubbers
paper of different sizes and colours

ready cut cards of different sizes
large paper for listing, wall charts
etc.
envelopes

Paper should be used on both sides then recycled. Scraps should be stored for later use. Find out about purchasing unbleached, recycled paper for your school.

Useful equipment for outdoors

whistle or bell
sturdy squares of cloth or plastic to
   sit on
clipboards
plastic pockets for survey sheets
   and non-permanent markers
magnifying glasses
specimen boxes (with magnifying
   lid)

hand nets (can be made from
stockings)
thermometers
containers with lids
compasses
binoculars
strong carry basket or back pack
   for materials

Other

camera
cassette player
a few musical instruments

References for teaching environmental education

Australian Conservation Foundation, *Habitat* (conservation magazine), ACF

Clyne, M. and Griffiths, R. *The Informazing Resource Book: Reading and Writing Non-Fiction* Nelson 1990

Cornell, J. *Sharing Nature with Children* Ananda 1979.

Curriculum Development Centre, Canberra. *Environmental Education: A Source Book for Primary Education* Canberra 1981

Dibella, M. & Hamston, J. *Under Cover: Exploring Values Education using Children's Literature* Collins Dove 1989

Dufty, Helen and David *Greenhouse Alert: A Learner's Handbook* Dellasta 1989

Fien, J. (ed.) *Living in a Global Environment* Australian Geography Teachers' Association 1989

Gould League & Victorian Association for Environmental Education *A Model Environmental Education Program: Warrandyte South Primary School* 1986.

Gould League *Environmental Games*

Gould League *Environmental Starters*

Gould League Guide to Protecting the Environment

(The Gould League also publishes other excellent material for primary environmental education. These include activity materials, survey materials, posters, stickers, field guides etc. A list of publications is available from to the Gould League Office in your state.)

Green Teacher (British journal) Available from Frances Hebblethwaite, Employ Publishing, PO Box 1042, Windsor, 3181

Greig, S., Pike, G. and Selby, D. *Greenprints for Changing Schools* World Wide Fund for Nature and Kogan Page 1989

Maefie, C. & Monaghan, B. *In Touch: Environmental Awareness Activities for Teachers, Leaders and Parents* Longman Cheshire 1989

New Scientist Gordon & Gotch, P.O. Box 29, Burwood 3125

NSW Association of Environmental Education. *Outlook Australia:*

Environmental Activities Martin 1989

NSW Dept of Education & Western Plains Zoo. *What's at Issue? A Range of Activities for Environmental Education* 1988

Ryan, F. and Ray, S. *The Environment Book* Macmillan 1991

Ryan, F. and Ray, S. *Green Hints* Green Press 1990

Schaefer, K. *Environment Explorer* Methuen 1985

Selby, D. and Pike, G. *Global Teacher, Global Learner* Hodder and Stoughton 1988

Tasmanian Environment Centre *A Sense of Humus: A Compost Program for Primary Schools* May 1988

Van Matre, S. *Sunship Earth: An Acclimatization Program for Outdoor Learning* American Camping Association 1979.

Van Matre, S. *Earth Education: A New Beginning* Institute of Earth Education 1990

Warren, G. *Animal Studies in School* (series) Burwood State College 1979/80

General references about conservation and the environment

Brown, L. *State of the World* Worldwatch Institute, Washington DC 1989

Carson, R. *Silent Spring* Pan 1960

Goldsmith, E. and Hildyard, N. (eds.) *Battle for the Earth: Today's Environmental Issues* Child & Associates 1988.

Lovelock, J. *The Ages of Gaia* Oxford University Press 1989

Malcolm, Steve. *Local Action for a Better Environment: Helping People to Get Involved* P.O. Box 453, Ringwood, 3134

Myers, N. (ed.) *The Gaia Atlas of Planet Management* Pan Books 1989

Rivers, P. *The Stolen Future: How to Rescue the Earth for Our Children* Merlin Press London 1989

Serventy, V. *Saving Australia: A Blueprint for Our Survival* Child & Associates 1988

Seymour, J. & Girardet, H. *Blueprint for a Green Planet* Angus & Robertson 1987

Useful contacts

APACE (Appropriate Technology & Community Environment) PO Box 770, North Sydney, 2059 (newsletter & many helpful ideas)

Australian Association for Environmental Education PO Box N157 Grosvenor Place, Sydney, 2000

Australian Association for Sustainable Communities 42 South Street, Fremantle 6160; and PO Box 621, Newcastle 2300

Australian Conservation Foundation 340 Gore Street Fitzroy, Vic. 3065

Conservation Centre of South Australia 120 WakefieldStreet, Adelaide, SA 5000

Earth Repair Foundation PO Box 15, Hazelbrook, NSW 2779

Earthwatch Australia 39 Lower Fort Street, The Rocks, Sydney 2000

Environment Centre of Victoria 247 Flinders Lane, Melbourne 3000

Environment Centre of WA 794 Hay St. Perth, WA 6000

Environment Centre of Tasmania 102 Bathurst St. Hobart, Tas. 7250

Environment Centre of NSW 39 George Street, Sydney, NSW 2000

Environment Centre of NT 24 Cavenagh Street, Darwin, NT 0801
Environment Centre of Canberra GPO Box 1875, Canberra, ACT 2601
Friends of the Earth: contact your local branch
Greenpeace Australia Private Bag 6, Broadway, NSW 2000
Men of the Trees: The International Society for the Planting and Protection of Trees 11 Pebbly Hill Road, Cattai, NSW, 2756
State Pollution Control Commission PO Box 367, Bankstown, NSW 2200
Wilderness Society 59 Hardware Street, Melbourne, 3000. Tel. (03) 670 5229